980.03 D74

Douglas, William O. 1898-

Holocaust or hemispheric co-op: cross currents in Latin

Greenville College
Library

GREENVILLE COLLEGE
ILLINOIS

From the Library of

Dr. Robert Millett

D0860329

Books by William O. Douglas

Towards a Global Federalism
Russian Journey
Beyond the High Himalayas
Almanac of Liberty
Farewell to Texas
Points of Rebellion
International Dissent
Holocaust or Hemispheric Co-op

HOLOCAUST
OR
HEMISPHERIC
CO-OP:

CROSS CURRENTS IN
LATIN AMERICA

980.03
D74

HOLOCAUST
OR
HEMISPHERIC
CO-OP:

CROSS CURRENTS IN
LATIN AMERICA

BY

JUSTICE WILLIAM O. DOUGLAS

RANDOM HOUSE

NEW YORK

Copyright © 1971 by William O. Douglas

All rights reserved under International and Pan-American Copyright Conventions. Published in the United States by Random House, Inc., New York, and simultaneously in Canada by Random House of Canada Limited, Toronto.

ISBN: 0–394–46272–6

Library of Congress Catalog Card Number: 71–140701

Manufactured in the United States of America
by The Colonial Press Inc., Clinton, Mass.

9 8 7 6 5 4 3 2

First Edition

Contents

143675

Prologue

There has been much talk over the years of hemispheric projects, of efforts on a hemispheric scale, of hemispheric reform and development. The Alliance for Progress was such a plan, based on Latin American ideas and on Latin American self-help and reform. It was not meant to be a U.S. program for Latin America.

After eight years of the Alliance for Progress there was an accounting.

The United States spent $8 billion. Latin America desired to industrialize. To do so she had to step up her imports of modern capital goods, technology, and managerial skills. These had to come mainly from the industrial nations, as they were only partially available from within the region. To import, Latin America had to be able to export. That is the basic way to increase foreign exchange.

But Latin America's position in world markets

deteriorated steadily in the Alliance years. That is why, once again, a new sense of crisis and a new spirit of dissatisfaction swept the region.

Coffee was Colombia's major export. In 1954 Colombia's coffee exports earned $550 million. In 1969, with a population larger by eight million persons than in 1954, Colombia exported more bags of coffee but earned no more than $320 million. Value of coffee exports dropped sharply, even though volume rose.

Furthermore, in 1954, a jeep cost approximately $1,400, or 14 bags of coffee. In 1969, a jeep cost approximately $2,300, or 43 bags of coffee. So, while the value of exports dropped sharply, the cost of imports rose sharply. At the same time, more and more barriers to Latin American exports were erected in the markets of the industrialized countries, and the acceleration of Latin America's own development became more and more difficult.

After eight years of the Alliance there was no favorable balance of trade for Latin America. As Dr. Carlos Sanz de Santamaria of OAS said, there was a favorable balance for the United States of more than $2 billion. "The Alliance for Progress, in other words, has been very good for the United States' economy and the U.S. Treasury."

This does not mean that hemispheric cooperation should come to an end. Rather, it indicates that efforts on a hemispheric scale must reach new dimensions, *entail other techniques, and be less limited* than what has been tried. That is the thesis which this volume will explore—a thesis that is contrary to the view that, because of the enormous difference in economic and political power between the United States and Latin American countries, true hemispheric partnership has become virtually impossible.*

One of the most prominent points of rebellion concerns the attitude toward the United States. We often have no understanding of Latin Americans. The words "liberal" and "conservative" have different connotations in Latin America than they have here. A Latin American "socialist" party may have as little to do with socialism, as "democratic," when used in Russia, has to do with democracy. "Marxist" in Latin America may mean no more than the epithet "Bolshevik" meant here after World War I when leveled against nonconformists.

We look down on Latin Americans, considering them inferior when they often have an excellence we seldom reach. There is great unhappiness on both sides of the Rio Grande over the relationship that exists. *Our hard-headed bankers have failed miserably.* The Washington bureaucracy, heavily conditioned by the regime of conformity which has pos-

* See Grunwald, *Latin American Economic Integration and the United States,* Brookings Institution, 1969.

[3]

sessed us, has been heavy-handed, timid, and seemingly unaware of the mounting volume of dissent welling up from below the Rio Grande. On the surface all seems well. But underneath is a smoldering distrust and even hatred. The Latin is an impeccably polite and suave person and seldom gives vent to his feelings in a confrontation. The image of the United States below the Rio Grande is not a bright one. The nature of that image helps block the vast renovation that Latin America needs if she is to enter the twenty-first century and share its wealth and carry the responsibilities that go with that status.

The suspicions and even the dislikes are bilateral. The Latins' reaction to us has often been described as a *love-hate* complex—a desire to have the material standard of living we enjoy and a repulsion against the ugly and uncouth manifestations of it. There is a like admiration of American technological efficiency and yet a fear of being exploited by it. This fear of American imperialism has *real* as well as *fancied* aspects. *Real:* If the industrial development comes through the installation of American companies, the nation's raw materials will not be primarily exploited for its citizens, but for foreigners. *Fancied:* Latin Americans fear that the United States is consciously or unconsciously afraid of a strong, vital Latin America. But our real concern about Latin America's population growth is not based, as some say, on a threat to our hegemony. A strong, thriving population would not weaken us; rather, it would improve hemispheric health and strengthen every component of that society.

The intensity of the anti-United States attitude will perhaps best be illustrated by a main function of CECLA—the Special Latin American Coordinating Committee. It is composed entirely of representatives of Latin American nations. It meets to discuss what position the various Latin American nations will take vis-à-vis the United States on specific issues. Our tactics have often been to divide those nations and thus increase our power. CECLA's strategy is to unite Latin America, if possible, and elevate its bargaining position against the neighbor to the north who is not always a good neighbor.

Kalman H. Silvert wrote in 1965:*

Latin America is a very difficult area to fit into extant theory. The range of cases is immense: twenty different republics with increasingly different histories are also characterized by vastly varied internal conditions. We must study migratory Indians and megalopolis, village economies and machine-tool industries, constitutional democracies and populist falangisms and mercantilistic dictatorships as well as village gerontocracies and institutionalized lawlessness. Latin America is the grave-

* 12 West Coast So. America Series, pp. 1, 21.

yard of simplistic and deterministic theories, of those schemes which hold that a nation which has "taken off" will automatically reach self-sustaining flight. It will not submit to simple notions derived without an adequate knowledge of the area's amazing store of data.

The problems presented by the region and its inhabitants are staggering; and the solutions can either make a man turn his back or set him dreaming. A romantic solution may indeed be the only viable one; and that is what I propose.

I

The Great Racial and Cultural Mix

The *campesino* in the Bolivian *altiplano*.

The great racial mix.

The Persian influence.

The hacienda system and its present vestiges.

It is a long way from the languid environment of the Caribbean to the stark, windswept, and severe *altiplano* of Bolivia. The Caribbean is for tourists, and the *altiplano* for mountaineers, as it rises up to 16,000 feet above sea level and is from 80 to 100 miles wide and over 500 miles long. There is a like diversity in Central America between the seashores and the high mountains. The high rolling basins of Ecuador and the savannahs of Brazil and Argentina have the mark of empires upon them, though from different worlds. The Andes, rising over 21,000 feet, are an imposing backdrop for the cherry orchards of Chile and the azure lakes of the Argentine. The jungles—now rid of yellow fever—have become hospitable. The wide and seemingly endless Amazon is still hardly explored.

There are many racial diversities—Europeans, Indians, Negroes, *campesinos.* The *campesino* in the *altiplano* is the Indian who was admitted to equality in the basic Bolivian Revolution of 1953.

Chicha, the beer of the *altiplano,* is made from corn and the *campesino* first places it in a gourd, then raises it to the sky, pours a good draught on the ground for Pachamama—god of the Incas—and drinks it down. Pachamama travels with the family of the *altiplano* even when they move to the jungle, for the Incas are not dead.

The Indian, who in Guatemala comprises 56 percent of the population, is in large part unassimilated, living in communities filled with suspicion and distrust. In many parts of Latin America the word "Indian" has the opprobrious connotation that the word "nigger" has in the United States. In Panama the Negroes and the Spanish have pretty well merged, at least 99 percent of all the people having some Negro blood. There is greater separateness in Brazil. While on the surface there is apparent harmony between blacks and whites, and while there are few hard-and-fast lines between the races, antagonism may well mount with a rising standard of living and an increasing competition for the good jobs.

In Latin America the architecture and social customs, even some wearing apparel, were greatly influenced by Persia. The Persians made up the court of the Arabs who conquered Spain, and it was they who made the cultural imprint on the Spaniards— who in turn unknowingly carried the imprint to Latin America. A Persian who entered a hacienda high in Ecuador or on the plains of Mexico would think he was in his own country.

Latin American society is paternalistic yet highly individualistic. Prestige attaches more to philosophers and poets than to engineers and merchants. There is a growing middle class in Latin America; but traditionally there has been no room for middle management—no place for managers of an industrial machine.

Historically, the hacienda, or estate, derived from a land grant that carried with it the right to the indentured labor of local Indians. The system was feudal in character: the *campesino,* or peasant, was supposed to work a specific number of days a week for the landowner, who in turn was supposed to see to it that the *campesino* got liquor for fiestas and decent burial for his family. At times, the landowner abused the relationship, working the tenant not on the hacienda but in his copper or tin mines, and pocketing the wages the worker would normally have received. Yet, cruel as the hacienda system was and remains, it is not usually carried to that extreme. *Campesino* and landowner are bound one to the other paternalistically. And so, when the modern corporation moves onto the scene, the personal element is lost and there may be chaos. Since the landowner was a patron who took care of the worker, why not the corporation? This problem gives new dimensions to collective bargaining and to the entire labor-management relation in Latin America.

The feudalistic nature of landownership in Latin America was illustrated in testimony by an expert before the Senate Foreign Relations Committee in 1968:

> I was on a large farm in Chile where the owner had tried and discarded an innovation that had been productive and successful. He had turned over

to many of his more favored workers pieces of land on a sharecrop basis on which they grew tobacco under direct contract to a commercial firm. Their incomes rose markedly and so did his. But as a result of their new affluence, they became, as he said, cheeky, and the whole social structure of his farm began to break down. The workers were no longer servile; they were no longer his peons; they were becoming independent operators. After a couple of years of this he reestablished the old extensive system, and stopped producing the more intensive crop, even though it had been more profitable. He made more money out of the tobacco, just as his sharecroppers did, but it was breaking down a social structure that he prized more highly than added income.

In Latin America the family is the strongest single influence. In the United States, we think of nepotism as scandalous; Latin Americans look on it more as a social duty. It is a breach of etiquette if one's second cousins are *not* taken care of. This is a spectacle that upsets the American "efficiency expert."

There are other problems in superimposing technology upon Latin American culture. The Latin American, like the Persian, has a high degree of fatalism. *Inshallah*—if God wills—is the Persian reply to an invitation to dinner, to a hunting party, to a reunion next year; *si Dios quiere*—if God wills—is the Latin equivalent. This philosophy extends into daily living—whether the automobile will break down, or the airplane will develop a weakness, or an industrial plant will go out of kilter.

In Latin America the main meal is eaten at noon, followed by a siesta. This habit, introduced into an industrial system, means not two traffic jams a day but four. Where else but home can a person go for a siesta? What accommodation is possible between the siesta and the automobile? There are signs that the siesta may give way.

II

Nationalism, Elitism, Modernization

The socioeconomic hierarchy in Latin America.

The pros and cons of feudalism.

Economic growth and demographic pressures.

Underemployment and unemployment.

The farm-to-city exodus.

Nationalism, elitism, modernization, and the need for change.

The Western Hemisphere mirrors the problems which affect peoples around the planet. What the United States does to put itself on a cooperative basis with Latin America can be the model for peoples elsewhere. If we can establish a détente in this hemisphere under which modern technology, coupled with a new value system, is allowed to make the lowly *campesino* prosperous, we are well on our way to working out world solutions to similar problems.

There is no reason why this cannot be done.

Latin America is a product of Spanish colonialism and of feudalism. John Hemming, in *The Conquest of the Incas,** tells how the cruel, heartless and evil regime of the conquistadors led by Pizarro laid low the Indians. Conditions in the plantations, silver mines, and mercury mines "ate up Indians like some demon god." There was no revolution for three hundred years. When Simón Bolívar, in a series of military victories from 1819 to 1825, won independence from Spain, the revolution ended. This revolutionary force spent itself in breaking Spanish rule. It did not extend to disrupting the social structure, uprooting the hacienda system under which agricultural lands were held, improving the status of the Indians, lessening the hold of the Catholic church by crea-

* Harcourt Brace, 1970.

tion of multi-religious communities, or redistributing the hold which the few had over the resources of the continent. Feudalism remained rampant.

There was, of course, change. In the last century and early in this century the middle class moved upward through a process of industrialization, notably in Mexico, Colombia, Argentina, Brazil, Chile, Uruguay, and Venezuela. But this movement, if measured by the degree to which it has absorbed the masses of the people in education, job opportunities, and the like, has largely been a failure.

The problem is intensified by the population explosion, due mainly to a decrease in infant mortality rates resulting from health measures. The population growth in Latin America is three percent a year, among the most rapid in the world. At the present rate of growth the population of Latin America will more than double by the year 2000. Its present population is 248 million, as compared to 234 million in the Soviet Union and 215 million in North America. By the year 2000, Latin America's projected population will be over 600 million—nearly as large as the projected Russian and North American populations combined.

Rapid population growth adversely affects the rate of economic growth in three ways: (1) Savings are reduced, little being left over after current consumption merely to stay alive; (2) Such savings as there are go into schools, hospitals, and housing, all of which have high payoffs in the long run and low payoffs in the short run; (3) High birth rates mean a larger proportion of dependent children in the population, and a smaller labor force relative to population.

One half of all Latin Americans are under twenty years of age. Life expectancy at birth is now sixty years, but nearly 64 percent of the people are under twenty-four years of age. More than four out of ten are less than fourteen years of age. This means that the relatively few people in the productive age groups have to produce enough to support the relatively numerous ones who are under- or overage.

Children have to be fed, clothed, and housed. They have to be given health services and must be educated and trained for the coming decades. Though this is the sector in which the Alliance for Progress was supposed to make its great contribution, it has failed miserably. The cost to the economy of educating and training people is very high, especially because these people do not contribute to the production process for many years.

The population explosion in Latin America has meant that, in spite of economic advances, the standard of living in some places on a per capita basis is lower now than it was twenty years ago. The impact is often more severe than population figures alone would indicate.

That so many Latin Americans are juveniles

means that the rate of economic growth must be accelerated way beyond what otherwise would be acceptable, if jobs are to be provided for those young people who annually reach the working age.

Latin American cities are unprepared to cope with their disastrous problems. Lima, capital of Peru, and Mexico City, capital of Mexico, are ringed with millions of people living in impoverished slums, without work, without food, without any of the comforts of life. When these problems occur on as large a scale as now, they result in what many Latins call "social decomposition."

The exodus from the farm to the city, which has caused this crisis, is more complicated than a mere escape from subsistence agriculture. The villages are dreary places and they always have been dreary. They offer none of the conveniences of life—no bright lights, no movies, no stores, no doctors. These traditional hardships are no longer accepted by the *campesinos*. The telling difference these days is in the news of another way of life, spread by radio, by tourists, and by other means of communication with the urban world. People leave the barren, windswept villages in which they have roots only of birth, not of ownership, to seek a better life. They may be misguided and unwise, but they continue to pour into the cities at a pace which will, I think, continue as news of the good life of the Haves reaches the

Have-Nots in increasing volume and intensity. If they all had TV sets, their dreary village life would soon appear to all to be unbearable.

The difference is the same one that Liu Shao-ch'i and Mao Tse-tung faced, starting in the 1950's. Liu said:

"In the socialization of agriculture, it is absolutely impossible for agriculture to attain collectivization without industrial expansion and without the realization of industrialization."

Under Liu's theory agricultural China would have reverted to the historical norm, increasing the authority of the rich landowners and shoving the rural masses into the category of landless and probably seasonal workers. This would have meant a drift to the cities and the large urban centers of China would have been ringed by the penniless, just as Lima and Mexico City are today.

The opposite line was taken by Mao Tse-tung, who said:

"In agriculture, with conditions as they are in our country, cooperation must precede the use of big machinery. . . ."

The story of the rural-urban struggle and the role played by the Red Guards in 1966 is told by Jan Myrdal and Gun Kessle, in *China: The Revolution Coninued.* *

* Pantheon, 1970.

[21]

So far as Latin America is concerned, new factories and an expanding industrial sector is not alone the answer. The answer is also in the modernization of the village itself. It must no longer be a place fit only for livestock; it must offer those amenities which lift a man above the status of a burro.

AID—the United States assistance program in Latin America—appears to realize this fact today. In the 40's, 50's, and 60's, however, the emphasis was on trade and manufacturing, not on humanism and village renovation.

In Latin America there is also mounting unemployment and increasing underemployment. Here again industrialization will not be their salvation. The industrialized nations are now at such a high level of technology that machines are going to produce more and more, as people produce less and less. This situation has already begun to give rise to a sense of enormous frustration. The problem is compounded in Latin America, where the average person being raised for the so-called modern society is poorly educated, if he is educated at all, and has inadequate, if any, economic opportunities. The mucilage that holds Latin American society together is gradually being eroded even without the realization on the part of the unemployed or underemployed that the arrival of the industrial society will mean not more work for him, but even less.

The transfer of population to the cities has been tragic from the economic point of view. In 1950, 53 percent of the population of Latin America was rural; by 1968, the rural population was down to 41 percent. In 1950, 35 percent of the nonagricultural labor force was employed in industry; in 1970, that proportion was down to 30 percent. In other words, 70 percent of the urban labor force was outside industry, either working in services or begging or stealing. Dr. Raul Prebisch of UNCTAD (United Nations Conference on Trade and Development) has estimated that even if an 8 percent GNP growth rate is achieved through the 80's, only 38 percent of the urban labor force will be in industry by 1990. In other words, it will take twenty years of extremely rapid growth to achieve an urban labor force which would approach the 1950 proportion.

Unless existing trade patterns are changed, an 8 percent rate of GNP growth is not attainable in Latin America. Herculean efforts are needed to improve the commodity export picture and to produce a Latin American common market. The Green Revolution, described in Lester A. Brown's *Seeds of Change,** marks the prospects of a phenomenal increase in wheat and rice production, out of the development of new varieties of seeds. But today, such a Green Revolution is still distant from Latin America. Even if it were achieved, an agricultural techno-

* Praeger, 1970.

logical revolution would produce a redundant labor supply of increasingly worse dimensions, unless there were a tremendously rapid economic and industrial growth at the same time.

Instead, what does seem likely is the prospect of violent urban unemployment explosions. The prospect is, in other words, one of revolutions that the intelligentsia, who believe in democratic traditions, may not be able to encompass.

The course of events in Latin America may indeed require revolutions if her societies are to be viable. The hostility of the United States to revolution is one force that stands in the way of basic change. That hostility, plus the essentially feudal nature of Latin American societies, combine to hold most of Latin America in an intolerable status quo.

Up until fifty or sixty years ago, the political system of Latin America was based on control by three institutions. The first was the army, which had military power. The second was the landowner, who had economic power. And the third was the church, which had moral as well as economic authority. This kind of political system, which may have been adequate for a feudal agricultural regime, is obviously unsuited to serve the needs of the coming era of technology. While the system has been modified, its basic essentials remain the same.

Nationalism has been a growing force in Latin America, but it has seldom been a revolutionary force. Only three Latin American nations have experienced basic revolutions since the colonial period: Bolivia, Cuba, and Mexico.

The confluence of revolutionary forces does not necessarily mean an Armageddon is inevitable, but great and new measures of extraordinary dimensions must be taken. The subsistence farmers and the urban poor—the so-called marginal ones—must, for the first time in Latin American history, be admitted into society. They must enjoy the benefits of full integration into the political and economic life of the several nations. Industry, schools, medical facilities, villages as well as cities, and modern agriculture must be made to serve the needs of all the people, not merely the top 20 percent who now receive most of the dividends of this bright and rich continent.

III

The Monroe Doctrine and the Forces for Popular Change

United States history.

The Monroe Doctrine.

OAS.

Cuba and the Dominican Republic.

Lyndon B. Johnson and counterinsurgency.

The needed U.S. policy goal—support of forces for popular change.

The proprietary attitude of the United States toward Latin America dates back at least to 1823, when President James Monroe announced the doctrine that non-American nations should not be politically active in this hemisphere or undertake military engagements here as these would be unfriendly acts toward us. At that time, Russia held Alaska and had forbidden foreign vessels to come within one hundred miles of those shores. Moreover, with Bolívar's victories in South America, it was feared that European nations would intervene in Central and South America to restore to Spain her former colonies or to acquire some for themselves.

Since 1823 not many decades have passed in which the Monroe Doctrine has not been applied to Latin American affairs. U.S. marines have landed on Latin American shores and our "gunboat" philosophy has aroused the people to the south of us. Beginning in the 1930's, in a series of agreements with nations of this hemisphere, we subscribed to the principle of nonintervention. In place of intervention there evolved, at least on paper, a principle of collective action against intrusions from overseas.

But, by the end of World War II, the danger to this hemisphere seemed to lie not in foreign invasion, but in the subversion of American governments by communism. By 1954, when a Pan-American conference was held in Caracas, it was declared that the "extension of communism to any American state would constitute a threat to the sovereignty and political independence of all, endangering the peace," and "would call for a meeting of consultation to consider the adoption of appropriate action in accordance with existing treaties."

In 1962, when Russia undertook to place long-range nuclear weapons in Cuba, President Kennedy set up a partial blockade of Cuba and demanded withdrawal of the Soviet missiles. This was a real confrontation and Russia yielded.

We had made an earlier, abortive effort to overthrow the Castro regime in the Bay of Pigs episode in April 1961. We now boast that we adhere to the policy of nonintervention and only act through the agency known as the Organization of American States (OAS)—except where our physical security is directly threatened, as it was in the Cuban missile episode.*

OAS, formed in 1948 at the Bogotá Conference, was ratified in 1951 and came into being as an embryonic regional United Nations. Its scheme of collective security was contained in the Inter-American

---

* Theodore Sorensen, in his book *The Kennedy Legacy,* ascribes the President's error in judgment vis-à-vis the Bay of Pigs to his heavy reliance upon the Pentagon and the CIA. "Thank God the Bay of Pigs happened when it did," he said, "otherwise we'd be in Laos by now—and that would be a hundred times worse." Kennedy's remedy for this mistake was to broaden his group of advisers to include "generalists" as well as "military and intelligence specialists."

Mutual Assistance Treaty of September 2, 1947, better known as the Rio Treaty. It was signed by the United States and nineteen Latin American countries, and reflected general acceptance of the principle of the Monroe Doctrine, in the sense that an attack on an American state by a non-American state would be considered an attack upon all. Under the treaty each state is obligated to assist in meeting such an attack, while awaiting measures of collective action by the entire group. This treaty has been construed by the United States to mean that the principles of the Monroe Doctrine are now extended to embrace collective security action, without restricting our right to take immediate action "in self-defense."

The Inter-American Mutual Assistance Treaty provides, in Article 3, that the parties agree that an armed attack "by any State against an American State shall be considered as an attack against all the American States, calling for collective self-defense." Article 6 provides that if "the inviolability or the integrity of the territory or the sovereignty or political independence of any American State should be affected by an aggression which is not an armed attack or by an extra-continental or intra-continental conflict, or by any other fact or situation that might endanger the peace of America . . ." measures of a collective nature may also be taken.

[31]

In 1954, the United States Congress passed a concurrent Resolution urging collective action by members of OAS to prevent any communist movement in the affairs of the States of the Western Hemisphere and, in particular, of Guatemala. There was no affirmative response south of the Rio Grande.

Numerous Resolutions were introduced in our Congress in 1961 calling for collective action in the Cuban situation, but none passed both Houses. On October 3, 1961, a Joint Congressional Resolution was enacted stating: "That the United States is determined—

(a) to prevent by whatever means may be necessary, including the use of arms, the Marxist-Leninist regime in Cuba from extending, by force or the threat of force, its aggressive or subversive activities to any part of this hemisphere;

(b) to prevent in Cuba the creation or use of an externally supported military capability endangering the security of the United States; and

(c) to work with the Organization of American States and with freedom-loving Cubans to support the aspirations of the Cuban people for self-determination.

Again there was no affirmative response south of the Rio Grande.

On October 22, 1962, the United States asked for cooperation in a blockade against shipment of Soviet weapons to Cuba. Nine nations agreed to help: Argentina with two destroyers; Honduras and Peru with troops; Costa Rica, Nicaragua, Panama, Guatemala, the Dominican Republic, and Venezuela with the use of their bases.

The truth is that the interventionist role of the United States has not changed, in spite of OAS. The U.S. financial interests in the Caribbean are so strong, the CIA is so active, and the American mind is so sensitive to leftist alarms that we are easily panicked. Our politicians still can make mileage on anticommunism. Our public servants—chilled by the memory of what Joe McCarthy did to the former China experts in the State Department—work hard to make a record indicating they leave no stone unturned to detect a communist. If we are to become a true partner with Latin America, our interventionist attitude must undergo a vast transformation.

The Dominican Republic produced crises in the 60's that make suspect the good intentions of the United States. Its first free election in thirty-eight years was held on December 20, 1962. Juan Bosch, an old friend of mine, won, despite the fact that during the campaign he was called a communist, some Catholic clergymen publicly denouncing him as such. But whatever Bosch's defects, he was far from being a communist. He was an intense nationalist;

he was very wary of Yankee "imperialism"; he disliked our military stance; he was to the left in Latin American politics in the sense that he was mildly socialistic; and being a poet, people called him a "dreamer." A combination of these forces brought him tumbling down in less than a year.

Less than a week after his election, Bosch was in my office in Washington, D.C. A toast to his great victory was in order; but since Bosch does not drink alcoholic beverages, we drank hot tea. The toast was not purely personal. Everyone was celebrating the "democratic" victory in the Dominican Republic. People who had no personal connections with the election were excited because communist Cuba now had, as a next-door neighbor, a democratic Dominican Republic which would really show the world what an underdeveloped nation could do under democratic leadership. I also had felt the contagion of that idea when Bosch won on December 22, and his presence in my office, as he told of his hopes and his plans, quickened my enthusiasm.

I learned later that he had come to me by reason of urgings from the State Department. Bosch was in general very suspicious of the Yankees, but he knew me and apparently thought I had no trace of "imperialism" in me. So it was gently suggested by our Latin American experts that he come to me for help and advice. Bosch said he had come to ask me a favor. I was then head of the newly formed Parvin

Foundation, which was dedicated to trying to plant seedbeds of democratic ideas in developing nations. Bosch asked me, Would the Foundation take on the responsibility of making all the *campesinos* literate? I said we would; and that was the beginning of a profound experience.

LeRoy Collins, former Governor of Florida, was then Chairman of the National Association of Broadcasters, and he and his assistant, John Perry, and others in his group were greatly excited by the bright prospects in the Caribbean. We had many talks and conferences about the Dominican literacy problem in Washington, D.C., in New York City, and in Santo Domingo. The problem was simple enough with a sympathetic government in power on the Island which owned the TV and radio stations; also, Rafael Trujillo—Bosch's corrupt fascist predecessor—had built community centers across the Island, the better to keep control of the people. LeRoy Collins and his group proposed to install a TV set in each center and radios in smaller meeting places. The Parvin Foundation, with the help of a group in Philadelphia that had done a TV literacy series there, would produce TV scripts in Spanish, teaching literacy in the environment of the agricultural Caribbean. Happily we found a Dominican who had a native genius as teacher.

We estimated that 85 one-hour TV shows would be needed to make a *campesino* literate in terms of his simple country needs. We went into production, completing 56 shows before Juan Bosch was ousted from the government seven months later. They were, I thought, superb productions. Indeed, they were so promising that we were already at work on the production of a weekly newspaper or magazine that would give these people something to read when they achieved literacy. When Bosch was ousted, the United States Ambassador, John Bartlow Martin, who had collaborated with us on the literacy program, sequestered the TV literacy shows; they were offered to all successive regimes but never used, and so far as I know, they are still secure in some U.S. depository.

In Santo Domingo, at the beginning of his term, Bosch asked me if I had time to sit with the committee drafting the 1963 Constitution. I replied in the affirmative; and there ensued a series of sessions that put the Caribbean in new perspective. My collaborators on the 1963 Constitution were men and women—all literate—who had been victims of Trujillo's atrocities. On the first day, the woman who sat next to me wore a sleeveless dress which revealed pockmarked arms. She in time told me that the scars were from Trujillo's cigarettes—one of his favorite methods of torture. I asked her the nature of her "transgression." It appeared that she and another lady had formed a circle which met once a week to pray for the end of the terror that possessed the Island. I asked her to describe that terror and she related many chapters. Political prisoners of Trujillo were often executed by hanging; and their bodies were taken from the gibbet to a deep-freeze that Trujillo had in his house. There the bodies were hung and displayed to male guests at state dinners when coffee and brandy were served.

This woman was tortured by cigarettes but never confessed. Her partner had been tortured differently—her long golden hair was set on fire with a torch; and she died of third-degree burns.

Male members of the Constitutional Convention told me similar stories, legion in number. In these men and women I sensed a spirit of release, of freedom, of triumph that I had never felt in any person in all my life. It was indeed the spirit of liberty that pervaded the entire Convention. The 1963 Dominican Convention was called "revolutionary," but it was indeed very much like our own Constitutional Convention: except that the powers of the Executive were more severely limited because of the Trujillo tradition that pervaded the history of the Island.

Until close to the end Juan Bosch was unaware that his closest adviser—closer than any party member or any cabinet officer—was a CIA man. Sacha Volman was his name, a clever Hungarian.

The insidious effect of this CIA penetration should be obvious. The CIA's deadly enemy is a communist; so its influence grows, as did Senator

Joe McCarthy's, by identifying every possible person as a communist. To the CIA, Juan Bosch was a "communist"; and it was therefore committed to his overthrow.

The modern account of the Dominican Republic is related by Ambassador John Bartlow Martin, whom John Kennedy sent to the Island. His account of the Bosch and post-Bosch days is given in his book *Overtaken by Events.** No one can put his finger on any single episode that marked the end of Juan Bosch. There was only a congeries of events. But I think that probably the most telling episode that made Bosch a marked man was his termination of a nefarious molasses contract which gave a New York syndicate of five individuals the privilege of buying all of the molasses of the Dominican Republic at 11 cents per unit, when the world price was 26 cents. The contract had been granted by Trujillo and had all the earmarks of being a corrupt bargain. I was with Juan Bosch when he tore up this contract.

"This is the kind of Yankee imperialism against which we are revolting," Bosch told me. I felt he was right; but when I read the prominent names that made up the New York syndicate, I foresaw trouble.

Repudiation of that contract—like other anti-Establishment moves by Bosch—was telegraphed to three sensitive powers: (1) U.S. financial interests,

* Doubleday & Co., 1966.

who saw the Banana Republics of the Caribbean as important opportunities for exploitation (and who had—and have—powerful connections in Congress, the State Department, the Pentagon and the CIA); (2) the Dominican Establishment, namely the church and business, who make any leftist a suspect and who in turn are tied in with local Joe McCarthy-type investigators who keep tab on all "communists"; and (3) the CIA and the Pentagon, which are out to "protect" all of us from what they regard as "communism." Part of the Pentagon's "achievement" was to increase the armed forces of the Dominican Republic to 25,000 men. "What are we supposed to do with all our newly formed power?" one Dominican colonel asked me. "Put down the people and their Juan Bosches?"

With the pressures of the rich and orthodox and power centers so great, it was not a surprise that Juan Bosch fell. He was replaced by a triumvirate picked by the army, and the Dominican Republic rocked along until the spring of 1965. Bosch—in exile in Puerto Rico and under round-the-clock telephone surveillance by the FBI—was running a campaign to be restored to power. Some army units rebelled, others stayed firm; the country was being torn asunder by an incipient civil war.

President Johnson decided that the Americans on the Island should be evacuated for their own safety; and our navy responded. To that extent we acted within the proprieties of international law. But then we broke our pledge under OAS not to intervene in the internal affairs of Latin American countries but to seek settlements through that organization.

One of the principles of OAS is stated in Article 5: "International order consists essentially of respect for the personality, sovereignty and independence of States, and the faithful fulfillment of obligations derived from treaties and other sources of international law."

No principle of international law permits one nation to invade another, without a state of war between the two. It must be put in those terms unless, of course, we are to make "international law" to fit our tastes as we go along. Unhappily, we have had a proclivity in that direction; indeed, that idea has become part of America's so-called manifest destiny.

OAS was too slow for us. On April 24, 1965, we sent marines and an air force unit to take control of the Dominican Republic; and they did. Johnson is reported by Ambassador Martin, in *Overtaken by Events,* to have said: "What can we do in Vietnam if we can't clean up the Dominican Republic? I know what the editorials will say but it would be a hell of a lot worse if we sit here and don't do anything and the communists take that country."

Juan Bosch, in explaining the U.S. attitude toward the Dominican Republic, spoke of the existence of "a military power directed by an association of bankers, industrialists, and military leaders who have their own plans to apply in any part of the world." * This powerful coalition needed a formula by which to work, as "aggressive wars" had been condemned at Nuremberg; and so the United States was forced to wage only "defensive" wars.

We soon had 8,500 occupying troops in Santo Domingo. On May 1, 1965, OAS, by a fifteen-to-five vote, had decided to send an inter-American force to the Dominican Republic. Honduras, Costa Rica, Nicaragua, El Salvador, and Paraguay sent token forces. Brazil sent 1,300 troops; and a Brazilian general took command of all inter-American forces, including those from the United States. OAS named a three-man mission to make peace—one member representing Brazil, one El Salvador, and one the United States—all three from nations which had sent troops into the Island.

What the United States did in the Dominican Republic was, like our action in Vietnam, an obnoxious form of intervention in the internal affairs of another nation. We sought to make this intervention palatable by hiding under the cloak of OAS, just as we used the cloak of SEATO to intervene in Vietnam. When Russia moved into Czechoslovakia in 1968, she too used a handy and available cloak, the Warsaw Pact. Czechoslovakia, far from being capitalistic, as the Soviet Union contended, was talking

* *Pentagonism: A Substitute for Imperialism,* Grove Press, 1968, p. 73.

about freedom. The Dominicans, far from being communist, were talking about removing themselves from the shadow of the United States.

In the spring of 1965, after we had invaded the Dominican Republic, President Johnson spoke at Baylor University:

> Out of the Dominican crucible the twenty American nations must now forge a stronger shield against disaster. The opportunity is here now for a new thrust forward to show the world the way to true international cooperation in the cause of peace and in the struggle to win a better life for all of us. . . .
>
> In today's world, with the enemies of freedom talking about wars of national liberation, the old distinction between the civil war and international war has already lost much of its meaning. . . .
>
> When the forces of freedom move slowly, whether on political or economic or military fronts, the forces of slavery and subversion move rapidly and they move decisively. . . .
>
> It is clear that we need new international machinery geared to meet the fast-moving events. When hours can decide the fate of generations, the moment of decision must become the moment of action. . . .

But Mr. Johnson saw the Caribbean as he saw Vietnam, as Texans of the last century viewed the Apache Indians. The "forces of slavery and subversion" in his eyes were those forces which challenge, erode, or frighten the establishment. That attitude—not peculiar to Johnson—makes the United States wholly suspect as a partner in Latin American affairs.

Dr. Richard N. Adams of the University of Texas has stated:*

> The United States has been basically afraid to permit real political variation. Such variation would inevitably mean the appearance of some socialist countries within the hemisphere. While the United States piously states that it wishes all men as rich as she, in getting down to the political and economic nitty-gritty, she knows that the U.S. taxpayer and consumer population would feel the squeeze if all of Latin America were somehow magically transformed into such a wealthy area.

The Dominican Affair proved that the position of the United States has really not changed since the days when we sent the marines into Central American nations. The Latins, knowing this, look on the United States with the greatest suspicion—excluding, of course, the members of the elite who own the wealth of Latin America.

Senator Frank Church, who chairs the Subcommittee on Latin America of the Foreign Relations Committee, said in 1970:

* *Survey of Alliance for Progress,* Subcommittee on American Republics Affairs, U.S. Senate Foreign Relations, p. 209 (1968).

One of the causes of political instability in the Caribbean is the widespread notion among ruling elites that in extremis the United States, because of our "send-the-marines" reflex, will step in to save oligarchic governments from violent overthrow. This only leads to dependency and irresponsibility in the basic sense of refusing to face and to solve the tough problems.

One difficulty is that we are preoccupied with counterinsurgency. When Johnson took over the Alliance for Progress, the emphasis of that program shifted from external threats to internal security. We not only built up the Latin American military, we set up police schools in the Canal Zone to which many people from Latin America were brought for training. We also spent large sums of money through the Alliance to equip local police and gendarmes. Soon the clubs used to crack the skulls of dissidents in individual countries were all marked "Made in the U.S."

Beyond these measures was the all-out counterinsurgency program led by the CIA. How many posts in Latin America are filled by the CIA, no one knows. But "revolution" has been made a dirty word, and even a populist is easily dubbed "communist."

The Pentagon's dabbling in sociopolitical research into internal warfare in Latin America, the better to know the conditions under which counterinsurgency must work, produced severe political re-percussions. Chile was selected for the project called Camelot, initially financed by a six-million-dollar grant by the army and run by a group of distinguished American sociologists. There Camelot had a brief beginning and a sudden end. When the Pentagon's connection with Camelot was discovered, it was denounced in Chile as an espionage plan. Then came the Dominican affair, and Camelot in the Latin mind became the symbol of U.S. interventionism and militarism, with the United States dedicated to the suppression of any revolutionary movement left of center.

The first requirement for the United States is to cease and desist this counterinsurgency. Revolutions are coming in Latin America and they will be as basic as the one in Bolivia or the one in Mexico. Revolution must be considered the norm, if social progress is to be made. Intervention, in the Johnson sense of the term, is utterly outdated.

The corollary is that once a government is formed—whether it be socialistic, communistic, or whatever—we must come to terms with it and do business with it and coexist with it in spite of ideological differences.

Senator Church recently said, "Never again should the United States unilaterally employ its armed forces within the hemisphere, except where, as in the case of the Cuban missile crisis, there is posed a clear and present danger to our national security—to the safety of the American people." *

The end of intervention is the only possible way to a real partnership with Latin America. The end of intervention makes mandatory the end of our support of counterinsurgency activities that now preoccupy us.

Castro's Cuba has little capability of subversion. The Soviet parties and the indigenous communist parties in Latin America are not virulent; nor are the pro-Peking parties, except in ideas. The principal threat to the status quo in Latin America comes from noncommunist populist forces which we help suppress through our support of Latin military forces, through Alliance for Progress, and otherwise. Senator William Fulbright said in 1968 that "because of our fear and obsession with the possibility of communist influence we have, for all practical purposes, brought social change and progress toward democratic processes to a standstill" in Latin America. In the same vein, Senator Wayne Morse said at that time that our grant of military aid to Latin America was "a stone around the neck of the Alliance for Progress."

To those who claim that if we give up counterinsurgency the Russians and Chinese will fill the void, there are three answers. First, those two nations

* *Congressional Record,* Nov. 11, 1969, p. S 14074.

have their hands so full in Asia and Europe that they are not going to have time for major work in this hemisphere. Second, there is no better defense against communist counterinsurgency than the encouragement of progressive democratic government—whether capitalistic or socialist. Third, while espionage and intelligence are comforting to the military and to governmental hierarchies, they undermine and impede our influence and moral authority. A great nation which extols an open society becomes greater if it lives up to the idealism of that kind of society.

Dr. Adams has further said:*

> The removal of U.S. support of counterinsurgency activities means that each Latin American country would have to come to terms with itself. This is probably the only way that the upper sector in Latin America will ever bend towards finding a better way for its own population to live. Revolutions are of great importance, because in the most difficult places, it will only be by actually breaking the control of the upper sector that some rapprochement, although perhaps not cordial, may be expected to occur. Revolutions will not be necessary everywhere, because after a few more, the idea will begin to diffuse. The mere fact that agrarian reform has been carried out in Mexico, Bolivia, and Cuba has made it an acceptable phrase to almost all

* *Survey of Alliance for Progress,* Subcommittee on American Republics Affairs, U.S. Senate Foreign Relations, pp. 209–11 (1968).

[47]

Latin American governments. One or two more revolutions, and it will cease to be a mere phrase and be hastened through as a fact, as a means of preventing further revolutions.

The Rockefeller Report, issued after the Governor made his tour of Latin America for President Nixon, sounds the alarum of communism and says that he who thinks it is no longer "a serious factor in the Western Hemisphere is thoroughly wrong." Many who live in haciendas or in plush apartments identify all discontent with communism. Communist ideas are everywhere; but so are the teachings of Jesus, Gandhi, Jefferson, and other great humanists. Communists are everywhere; but so are anti-imperialists and socialists. The forces of discontent will in time rally under banners not carried today in many Latin American nations. We of the north will have no greater ability to select these standards than we have in Vietnam. Our only contribution can be toward eliminating or alleviating the conditions that give rise to blood baths and the liquidation of people à la Russia or à la Spain.

The important question is how much time is left for those who seek a restructuring of Latin American society without blood baths or the liquidation of any class. Some are so optimistic as to say ten years. Most knowledgeable people guess that less than that will be required. No one, of course, knows. But those Latin Americans who walk in the cooperative tradition of Martin Luther King—and there are thousands of them—do not have much time. North and South America face a grave emergency.

The black-or-white posture of the Rockefeller Report reflects little reality. The Governor's thought that "a Castro on the mainland, supported militarily and economically by the Communist world" would present "the gravest kind of threat" may or may not be true. Communism would be abhorrent in the United States. But communism in Latin America need not necessarily be the Stalinist, malignant type. A Yugoslavia south of the Rio Grande would not menace its neighbors; nor would the kind of Czechoslovakia which Dubček sought to evolve. We must grow up and become mature enough to realize that we do not need only capitalistic and free-enterprise neighbors to live peacefully in an international cooperative order.

The Rockefeller Report recommends the creation of a Western Hemisphere Security Council "to cope with the forces of subversion that operate throughout the Western Hemisphere." As one reads the account, this "Security Council" sounds pretty much like an International Un-American Activities Committee. Dominated as it would be by the United States and the host of dictators we have helped create, it would be intolerable. To repeat, people south of the Rio Grande are already highly suspicious of us. This new Security Council would take over from OAS; and OAS has come to signify the cruel crushing of change and progress in the Dominican Republic. If we want to keep such friends as we still have in Latin America and to speak in a voice of compassion and understanding, we cannot make hemispheric internal security our concern. Senator Morse said: ". . . a discussion in the Rockefeller Report about the threat of communist subversion is a rationalization for strengthening military operations and regimes in Latin America."

The governments in Latin America that see things more or less "our way" are Somoza's in Nicaragua and Stroessmer's in Paraguay. Are they not better allies, people ask, than Mexico, which is strong in the democratic faith? After all, Mexico is very often opposed to our policy. How many Mexicos, they ask, could we tolerate?

If there were twenty-three Mexicos in Latin America, we would not have unanimity on all issues. But we would have the basis for an enduring partnership, just as we do with the States in our own Union. Mississippi and Oregon are far from identical. But they get along—coexist in the international sense.

IV

The Military and the Elite

The maldistribution of income in Latin America.

The military and the elite in Latin America.

That military and elite mirrored in the United States:
the Pentagon and the CIA; the necessity for U.S.
removal of military missions.

Today the United States is the great support of the Latin American elite. The enormity of our undertaking is shown by the overall facts. Taking Latin America as a whole, 50 percent of the people live below the subsistence level, pretty much as cattle; 30 percent receive wages which permit marginal living; 20 percent own the wealth and are the affluent members of this old and proud civilization. More specifically, 60 percent of the population obtains only 19 percent of Latin America's total personal income, whereas 5 percent of the population obtains 31 percent of the income.

The poor are the most difficult for the outsider to know. As stated in the Rockefeller Report:

"The *campesino* goes to bed hungry every night of his life. He will probably never see a doctor, a hospital, a dentist, or a nurse. He has little hope of being vaccinated against smallpox, or inoculated against typhoid, tetanus or yellow fever. If he becomes ill, there is no medicine; he trusts to fate that he will either get better, or die."

Moritz Thomsen, a former Peace Corps member in Ecuador, writes in *Living Poor* * that these people have qualities of "heroism and endurance," of "a wild and savage strength." They are miserably poor and remain that way. Yet somehow or other they survive, though certainly their diet is so protein-deficient that their brains never fully develop. Being il-

* University of Washington Press, 1969.

literate and ignorant, they are unaware of the forces that shape their destiny. Yet it is national policy to keep them poor, primarily to tap the unlimited supply of cheap labor so attractive to the industrialist. But the main pressure to maintain poverty comes from the hacienda owners or other landowners who have a one-crop commodity export and need to squeeze labor to make a handsome profit. They are indeed plantation-minded, in the pre-Civil War U.S. sense of the word. And we—the great moneyed interest of the continent—are on their side, not on the side of the masses.

If the 20 percent who constitute the elite are to remain on top, a large degree of coercion is required. Their power depends upon the constant generation of the idea that to change is dangerous. The military moves in an ever-recurring cycle to keep the pieces fastened together in most Latin American countries, though a few, notably Costa Rica, are free of this problem.

Military control may be largely through veto power, as in Chile, Uruguay and Venezuela. Or, as in Colombia and Ecuador, there may be a sharing of power between military and civil authorities, with the military having complete autonomy over its own affairs and a degree of veto power over civil matters. In Bolivia, in the Central American states (except Costa Rica, Santo Domingo and Haiti), in Brazil,

Argentina, Paraguay and Peru, the military control is less subtle and more overt.

The military is less powerful whenever the 20-percent elite has a consensus of the people, as it does in Chile and Mexico. But if that elite is to have stability without consensus, it must employ the military to keep the economic, financial, and social structure intact.

While the military does service for the civilian oligarchy that owns Latin America, it really has little social identification with the elite. The officers are predominantly lower middle class in origin. Their instincts are for stability; and they have a fear of social upheaval. Thus they are cautious and conservative.

The military regimes in Argentina, Brazil, and Bolivia govern nearly half of the entire population of Latin America. They proceed on the premise that civilians, with their political parties and institutions, are inefficient and corrupt and that the military alone is capable of governing. They are dedicated not only to keeping the lid on social upheaval tightly fastened, but to eradicating fiscal mismanagement and to promoting modernization.

The Pentagon has a natural affinity for these Latin American military groups. The urban middle class origin of the Latin American military plus its authoritarian education makes it status quo oriented; and certainly it is anticommunist, in the gross sense of the term, being opposed to the growth of popular movements which might result in the formation of strong independent centers of power. This makes the military law-and-order oriented, and ready to accept modernization but oppose development. That is to say, the military is for improving the standards of consumption of the urban middle class—more automobiles, more jewels and furs for wives and mistresses, better doctors and dentists, and the like. But it is against development, e.g., the release of 80 percent of the people from the bondage in which they are held.

This status quo orientation makes the Latin American military extremely palatable to the Pentagon, which instinctively, and for public relations purposes, fears being associated with change, not to mention revolution.

Senator Jacob Javits recently described the erosion of good will we have suffered as a result of our military stance in Latin America:*

> The fact is that we have alienated large segments of the civilian population in various Latin American countries, that antimilitary political groups have rioted against the United States as a symbol and even against our Presidential emissary to express their discontent with our policy and with their

* *Congressional Record,* Oct. 13, 1969, p. S 12354.

own military governments. This has resulted in a serious loss of influence by the United States on many major issues.

When we started Alliance for Progress, 180 million Latins were living under *civilian* regimes. By 1970, 140 million of that group were living under some form of *military* dictatorship.

Overall, the military in Latin America is an antidemocratic force. Without its restraining influence, populist governments would probably be in power in most Latin American countries. Whether right or left, they would probably be not democratic, in our sense, but authoritarian. Yet a populist regime would probably advocate social reform at a more rapid pace than the military has ever espoused. It is mounting civilian resistance to military domination that promises to mark the years ahead.

As this is written there are signs that the military junta that has Peru in its grasp is moving left. At the meeting of the Inter-American Development Bank in Punta Del Este, April 1970, General Francisco Morales Bermudez, Peru's Minister of Finance, rejected both capitalism and communism as paths for developing nations to follow. Rather, he advocated state planning and control which obviously is a form of socialism. It is not yet known whether this is symptomatic of a new trend.

However fascist the ideology of the Latin military, the Pentagon—plus its CIA affiliate—has an affinity toward it. The Pentagon has large amounts of surplus military supplies to sell or dispose of—not nuclear bombs, but tanks, air reconnaissance planes, machine guns, and fighter planes. The Latin military uses its military equipment not against foreign invaders but against the local people, so that the Pentagon's supply fits the Latin demand. It should be noted that about 7 percent of the advances under Alliance for Progress were for military hardware and supplies.

The United States has military missions in seventeen Latin American countries: Argentina, Bolivia, Brazil, Chile, Colombia, Costa Rica, the Dominican Republic, Ecuador, El Salvador, Guatemala, Honduras, Nicaragua, Panama, Paraguay, Peru, Uruguay, and Venezuela. Each of these missions includes army, navy, and air force; and the complement of men making up these missions totaled nearly eight hundred, though the Pentagon promised to cut it in half by June 30, 1971.

These groups—known as Latin Milgroups—are under the Southern Command (Cincsouth), which is located at Quarry Heights, Panama Canal Zone, under the command of a four-star general. In Panama we have an additional 4,000 soldiers.

It is commonly said in Bolivia that the 1964 coup by René Barrientos that deposed Victor Paz Estenssoro was inspired by our military mission. And the same charge is made in Brazil respecting the Castelo Branco coup that ousted João Goulart in 1964. But both rumors are strictly denied. It is commonly claimed that our military missions are set up to teach the Latin military that civilian authority should always be dominant. But the record shows we have not done that.

The Pentagon finds these missions extremely useful. There are colonels and majors not quite up to snuff, yet with powerful political backing. What better way to allot second- and third-rate officers to active duty overseas than to put them into these military missions? These missions are, however, large and expensive to the American taxpayer. In Latin America it is a standing joke that one of our military missions supervising a $500,000 military budget one year cost $600,000 to operate.

The first contribution by the United States to Latin American development would be the complete withdrawal of all of our military missions, leaving any residual tasks to our military attachés. And the Cincsouth military operation should also be liquidated. No American military mission would any longer outshine the American ambassador; civilian control over foreign policy would be restored. Although no basic problems would be instantly solved by this new, political orientation, it would be a start toward reaffirming the predominantly civilian spirit of our Constitution and toward demilitarizing our approach to Latin America. At least we, the people of the United States, would not be fostering military solutions to the staggering problems in the bright lands to our south, or encouraging default in their solution by bolstering the status quo through coups by military junta.

V

The Contradictions of Technology and the Anomaly of Mass Consumption

The Beginnings of the Alliance for Progress.

The shortcomings in its philosophy.

The manner in which we have strengthened the already-established regimes.

The tragedy of the philosophy of dollar aid.

The role of private enterprise and its limitation.

The contradictions of technology and the anomaly of mass consumption.

Planning by whom and for whom?

The Alliance for Progress showed bright promise at the start. Ted Moscoso, a brilliant Puerto Rican to whom I had given the oath of office, was its administrator. Knowing Latin America, he had thought that the place to start his program was with the renovation and modernization of the villages.

At that time, I gave him a dinner at my home; the only other guest was Dr. James Yen, whose Mass Education Movement I will discuss later. Jimmie talked eloquently of his experiences in China, Formosa, and the Philippines, and Ted asked questions and probed deeply. Finally, at about midnight, Ted stood up, embraced Jimmie, and said that this educational program was basic in Alliance for Progress.

For a year and a half Ted did his best to get his bureaucracy headed in such a direction. Jimmie spent days talking with the officials; but one day, a year and a half later, he called me in the Far West, saying the effort had failed because the Alliance for Progress staff was geared to Marshall Plan philosophy as applied in Europe—build up the middle class, erect plants, put people to work, and the rest will take care of itself.

But Europe had a viable democratic base and Latin America did not. The only base in Latin America was the elite; while this group wanted money, they were not architects of new institutions and political revolutions.

When President Kennedy asked me in 1962,

"What's wrong with Moscoso?" I replied, "Nothing. The thing that is wrong is with Ted's staff. It is Marshall Plan-oriented." It was an old, able staff, oriented to the giving of aid in order to create a new bourgeoisie overseas, who in turn would be bastions of strength against communism. That meant programs of aid for the elite, not for the masses. It meant markets filled with luxury goods for the elite.

In agriculture the productivity of workers is very low, even nominal. When agriculture experiences the technological revolution the present redundant labor supply in agriculture will multiply. That will give new urgency to industrial development.

Neither industry nor agriculture is geared to the mass needs of Latin America. The agricultural sector does not produce enough to feed the rest of the economy. While a robust agricultural sector should help stem inflation, its stagnation encourages inflation through the rise in agricultural prices leading to wage increases elsewhere. Moreover, although agriculture does provide some export earnings, Latin America also must import agricultural products. Renovation is needed in all sectors of the economy.

One who travels the world can, in Athens, Istanbul, Karachi, Saigon, and on east, see American aid dispensed on the "trickle down" theory. That is to say, to feed chickens, we should give oats to the horses.

Where 50 percent of the people are outside of the

economy, barely existing, and another 30 percent live on marginal wages, there is no mass market for goods produced by private enterprise. The only market is among the 20-percent elite and that is a market having no relationship—or precious little—to the emergence of a society from feudalism to political and economic democracy.

Political changes in Latin America are beyond the ken of those of us who move in the Western tradition. These changes will come, but we are the least qualified to write the prescription for them. The U.S. theory that money will do everything is simply not true. Our fixation on that theme gives a tragic turn to our Latin American policy. Our concern with dollar values assures the elite of Latin America that we will not allow their regimes to collapse in the economic or political sense. Those regimes will, it is understood, be preserved. If they knew that their futures rested on their own inventiveness, important reforms would doubtless be instituted. But the United States, as underwriter, keeps Latin America from turning that corner.

Sumner Welles, speaking for the State Department, said in 1943 that, as respects Latin America, the United States "reflects in its foreign policy the objective of its domestic policy, namely, improvement in the standard of living in which all elements will participate, but particularly those heretofore ill-clothed, badly housed, and poorly fed." Through the years this has been, off and on, our ideal; but it is an ideal that has seldom been realized in practice —as witnessed by the Alliance for Progress, established under that pretense, whose actual performance was in the main very different.

In fact, as a result of Alliance for Progress, the rich got richer and the poor, poorer—and few basic reforms were achieved. This may indeed be the long-range tendency when private enterprise becomes the sole implement for the public good. For example, Ifigenia Navarrete of the University of Mexico has shown in her studies that forty years after the 1920 Revolution in Mexico—

(1) Five percent of the families received 37 percent of the personal income. Fifty-seven percent of the personal income accrued to the "wealthy class";

(2) While the percentage of people receiving less than average income decreased from 70 percent to 65 percent, those in the lowest 20 percent suffered a relative decline;

(3) While the percentage of families receiving average income increased from 18 to 19 percent, those receiving an income greater than average increased from 12 to 16 percent;

(4) Entrepreneurs increased their average income by 70 percent, salaried people by 13 percent and agrarian wage earners by 10 percent, while non-agrarian workers experienced a decrease in average income of 6 percent.

From the point of view of the industrial countries, the developing nations, or Third World, become the potential mass market for goods, products, and processes which the members of the affluent society first produced only for themselves. These technological goods and services, however, frequently benefit the producers more than the consumers. Under the industrial revolution, which has been on us full force for less than one hundred years, packaged solutions to basic human needs have been prepared; and it is almost a religion with us that man's God-given needs are for packages which we and other members of the industrial bloc have invented. These products come in the same packages whether they are supplied by capitalistic, communistic, or cooperative industrial societies. This extends to replacement parts, which in practical effect furnish a long-range, continuing loyalty to the same old producer of the industrial machine.

Four of the major civilizations—the Western world, Japan, the Soviets, and Eastern Europe—have assumed a quasi-technological form. Their prevailing philosophy is that technological innovations, whether or not centrally controlled, are the measure of the public good and result in man's fulfillment.

It may be that, in time, all nations will be rich and benevolently endowed with traffic jams, overcrowded hospitals, and packed classrooms. A recent study showed that our present rate of production, if continued until 2000 A.D., would give us 232 million automobiles, i.e., 700,000 miles of highways with cars bumper to bumper.

The interim period for Latin America is agonizing. It takes valuable foreign exchange to get one automobile into Brazil from Europe, Russia, or the United States. And that one car probably thwarts the plans of some dozens of people to get good bus transportation, for buses, too, must be purchased with foreign exchange. On another level, a stranger traveling the outback of Latin America might honestly think that the best gift to a villager would be a brand new American refrigerator. Yet, the cost of getting a refrigerator to one family would set back the plans to get a community freezer that would serve the entire neighborhood.

What is true at the level of consumer goods is also true at the level of medical care. The great thrust in Latin America is toward the establishment of specialized nursing, pharmaceutical, and medical schools. This again is a part of the rationale that the developing countries should grow in the image of the industrialized nations. Yet Latin America needs midwives and first-aid trainees who know how to work without the supervision of an official physician. Latin America is pushing for modern hospitals; and that is fine. But in terms of priorities, it needs safe water systems first.

In Latin America roughly 35 million people in

urban areas and 100 million in rural areas are without potable running water. Out of this condition come typhoid and the diarrheal diseases for which modern medicine and plush hospitals have few preventive measures. Potable water supply systems bringing treated water to the home are a basic health requirement.

It is in such respects as these that the Alliance for Progress was controlled to a great extent by an unsophisticated state of mind. The goods and services tendered were for members of the affluent culture. They were far, far beyond the reach of the masses, even in terms of a future generation or two.

That was at one time the prospect for China's regime because, as we shall see, in the early fifties the village had the lowest priority, and urban centers the highest.

Dr. Salvador Allende, President of Chile, said in 1970 that capitalism had not been able to solve the social and human problems of Chile with particular reference to "problems of jobs, food, housing, education, health, and rest and recreation."

Overseas, Coca-Cola, Pepsi-Cola, hamburgers, and comic books are symbols of American culture. The introduction of a Coca-Cola plant may be modernization in terms of a special limited view but it is not development in terms of the needs of the people of Latin America. And while the construction of a teachers' training school along the North American pattern might be taken as a sign of progress up here, in Latin America it might well be a sign of retrogression and not responsive to the basic needs of the miserable 80 percent who make up the deep and festering bottom of Latin American society. The higher one goes in schooling, the more distant and withdrawn he becomes from the mass of society he is supposed to serve.

Jan Myrdal and Gun Kessle, in their book *China: The Revolution Continued,** make clear that it was one role of the Red Guards in 1966 to turn back the tide of control by learned cadres in China and place that control in what we call "the town meeting."

A vast amount of planning is needed by the architects of the new Latin American society. If the present elite do the planning, they will subconsciously or purposefully use the masses as the foundation on which to build an affluent society for themselves. The planning must be done by Latin Americans who are genuinely concerned about all their people; and since all plans require money and since much of that money will come from the outside, it is well that it come through multinational agencies. If it does, the advice and orientation will be less parochial, more flexible, less orthodox. Then plans will not be anchored to the self-interest of a syndicate whose basic aim may be to flood an area with the Volkswagen or the Ford.

* Pantheon, 1970.

Planning for an area where 80 percent of the people are destitute means more—much more—than planning to make them consumers of the packaged goods of the United States, Europe, Japan, or Russia. Planning means basic decisions that only free and imaginative local people can make:

(1) Should we spend our foreign exchange on (a) buses for the multitudes rather than private cars for the few, (b) a community deep-freeze rather than individual refrigerators, (c) a community TV rather than individual sets, (d) motor vehicles designed for travel over rough and gutted roads, or modern freeways?

(2) Gold still piles up in the Church though in northeast Brazil, say, the people are destitute. Are pure water supplies and refrigeration for fly-infested meats more important than additional golden altars?

(3) Should a medical school be established, or alternatively should ways be found of providing a safe supply of drinking water either (a) by protecting each well from surface drainage, or (b) by piping water into each home? Jorge de Ahumada, Chilean economist, has observed, in this connection, that every dollar spent on doctors and hospitals costs one hundred lives, in that the same amount if spent on safe drinking water would save that many people.

(4) Should a North American school system be

installed or should a wholly new start be taken along the lines of (a) a crash literacy and trade school program for adults, and (b) a grade school education aimed not at producing enrollments at distant universities but at developing special skills as artisans, artists, potters, and technicians?

VI

The Anatomy of Bolivia

Indian poverty in Bolivia.

The need for economic and social justice, particularly employment, in Bolivia.

Communists in Bolivia.

The need to revitalize the mines.

Why should not Bolivia have a tin refinery?

The role of the Maryknoll Fathers and the need for credit and other co-ops.

How can people be adequately educated to the needs of a "developed" society?

Is it not only education in pollution and in frustration?

Before an underdeveloped nation can make such basic decisions as we have discussed, it probably must have a basic revolution. Few North Americans—and I fear, not many Latin Americans —really understand what such a revolution in the democratic, noncommunist tradition entails. It may be helpful to look at the anatomy of such a revolution.

That is why in the mid-sixties I went to Bolivia. I traveled through most of that country, seeing the jungles as well as the *altiplano,* and interviewing *campesinos* as well as the civilian officials and the military.

The *altiplano* of Bolivia is a high plateau that lies between 12,000 and 16,000 feet above sea level between the vast Cordillera Occidental mountain range on the west, and the Cordillera Real on the east. This tableland, eighty to one hundred miles wide and over five hundred miles long, is a dry, windswept, treeless land (though the eucalyptus recently has been introduced). Lake Titicaca is set like a jewel in this vast, dreary expanse, a huge sapphire one hundred thirty-eight miles long and seventy miles wide, extending into Peru. Three fourths of Bolivia's four million people live on the *altiplano.*

In the days of the Hoover Administration, landlocked salmon were planted in Lake Titicaca and rainbow trout in lesser lakes and streams, in order to bring protein to the diet of the people. The fish prospered to such an extent that a thirty-five-pound salmon is common in Titicaca and an eight-pound rainbow in the other waters. For those who come down from the United States this is a fisherman's paradise. Distant snow-capped peaks in the 20,000-foot zone lift the heart, though the thin air of the *altiplano* slows the newcomer to a walk.

In spite of the thin air and austere conditions, the bulk of the Bolivian population has lived in the *altiplano* for centuries. Drab adobe huts dot the plateau. The soil is thin; the environment grim. The *altiplano* is raw in the wet season; but the real cold comes between May and November, when there are no rains and when the thermometer often drops below freezing at night and rises to 75 degrees by day. Potatoes as small as walnuts are grown, as well as corn and a millet known as *quinoa*. A family may have llamas or alpacas or a few sheep, herded by children during the day and enclosed within a stone corral at night. The land is brown except during the rains, and crop failures are common; man lives on the edge of subsistence.

Just below the *altiplano,* on the periphery of the mountains, are high valleys known as the *yungas.* They are veritable cloud factories in the wet season and the area that produces most of the coca, whose leaves are chewed for cocaine. Here nearly a fifth of the people live.

To the east and north is the jungle, starting about

five hundred feet above sea level and rising around three thousand feet, in the hill country known as the *alto Beni.* The jungle historically has been hostile and forbidding. Until recently it offered death through malaria or yellow fever, but now the success of malaria control is evident everywhere; practically every building has the proud sign SNEM (Seruicio Nacional de Erradicacion de la Malaria) indicating it is regularly sprayed for mosquito control. The jungle was remote because it was roadless. Parts of its trackless expanse still hide cannibals. The jungle, vast and unexplored, lay beyond the zone of the Incas and the Spanish who followed. The *altiplano,* the *yungas,* and the lower fertile valleys in the eight- to nine-thousand-foot zone, such as Cochabamba, were the home of practically all Bolivians.

There were historically no schools, no first-aid centers, no hospitals, in the *altiplano* or *yungas.* Worse than that, the Indian, under his Spanish masters, was a serf. He owed the hacienda owner three to four days' free labor a week and his womenfolk were subject to call for all household duties in the big house. No wages were paid, the Indian raising the food he needed for himself on designated tracts. The Spaniard came to Bolivia not to work but to live in style, by European standards. When gold and silver were discovered, the Indian was conscripted to work the mines. He was a slave, all legalism aside, and when the arduous work killed him off, the Spanish owner imported slaves from Africa, who died like flies in the thin air of the *altiplano*.

In the sixteenth century, Potosí, a barren, cone-shaped hill about 16,000 feet high, was mined for silver. Now, though the silver is exhausted, five thousand shafts pierce the mountain, to mine the tin that formerly was discarded.

The tailings are so rich in tin that they are worked by over 2,000 cooperatives, as well as many contractors. The acreage they work is defined by contract; and the profit incentive is strong.

The tailings, however, are not the only source of profits in tin. In the days of the Spanish, tin was so valueless that it was mixed with mud, like ordinary rock, to make adobe blocks. The Prefect of Potosí, General Garron, told me that, without doubt, many adobe houses in Potosí contain fortunes in their walls. I asked how he could be so sure. He said that about twenty-five years ago the owner of one of the old, grand houses of Potosí decided to remodel it for his daughter. At the start of the remodeling, workers found each adobe block filled with tin metal.

"He ended up," the Prefect said, "selling all the adobe in the old, grand house for enough money to build a modern one."

In all, at least three billion dollars' worth of silver was taken out of Potosí. Though it went mostly to Spain, silver was so plentiful that when a figure of a saint was moved from one cathedral to another in the town of Potosí, the cobblestones were taken up and replaced with silver ones. Slave labor brought the ore up rope ladders in fifty-pound packs and llama trains packed it to Pacific ports. Rafters were needed in the mines; and huge mahogany timbers were desired for building the mint at Potosí, now fully restored as a museum. Mahogany was available only several thousand feet lower down and many dozen miles distant. The huge wooden pillars still on display in the old mint were brought up on the backs of men.

The grand houses of Bolivia were once at Potosí. Pianos from England, furniture from France and Spain, were packed in by llama. The theater and the arts flourished. Down the valley, at Sucre, a great university was established long before the Pilgrims reached our shores. The revolt against Spain, which started in 1809 and finally succeeded in 1825, was sparked at Sucre by the Bolivians, who were inspired by Thomas Jefferson and our Declaration of Independence. Their Declaration of Independence lists their grievances against their king, as does ours; but, in true Latin spirit, it starts off with the words "Furiously complaining."

Their list of grievances, however, did not speak for the Indian. The revolution led by Simón Bolívar did not end the awful serfdom on which Bolivia rested, any more than our Revolution ended slavery. It took Abraham Lincoln and the Civil War in this country to accomplish that, as it took Victor Paz Estrenssoro and his revolutionary party (known as MNR) to bring to an end Bolivia's exploitation of the Indian. But the end did not come until April 1952. In that year modern Bolivia was born. The ancient hacienda system was abolished; land was distributed to the Indians; major mines were nationalized; the franchise was extended to all men and women; the word "Indian" (*indio*) was obliterated, *campesino* taking its place; a grass-roots democracy in the Jacksonian sense was created; overnight an ancient feudal regime faced up to twentieth-century problems.

With the breakup of the feudal system, reconstruction was necessary. Towns had no pure water supply. Most areas had no schools. Roads were limited; old ones needed extension and modernization. Railroads and airports had to be built. Hospitals and first-aid centers were in great demand. And why not open up the jungle, where crops would grow lush, and resettle the *campesinos* of the *altiplano* there? Why not put the army to work on these projects, to participate in the social and economic revolution underway?

There has long been a rapport between Bolivia and Israel. In the late 1930's and early 1940's, when Hitler was bent on his program of extermination, Bolivia opened her doors and 5,000 Jewish families settled there. Many remain today. After the 1952 Revolution, Israel became a dynamic symbol in Bolivia. Among other things, the Israeli army produced men with a plow in one hand and a gun in the other. Bolivians went to Israel to see that army; and they were greatly impressed. Why should an army merely stand guard or fight? Why not lend a helping hand in civilian reconstruction?

This was the way that Civic Action—as Bolivian military participation in social and economic reconstruction is called—was born. Four battalions were assigned to the program, with United States army officers as technical advisers. Bolivian officers were in command; but they worked not only with their American military counterparts, but also with American AID, the American Peace Corps, United Nations experts, Israeli technicians, and any and all others who offer foreign assistance in the democratic tradition. The theory was that "a nation of small farmers will never go communist."

In 1960, colonists from the *altiplano* began to arrive in Santa Ana, on the Rio Beni. I went to see this resettlement project, which is connected with La Paz by a 140-mile road. A good gravel airport puts it only twenty minutes distant by air.

To begin with, the Civic Action program gave the settlers health examinations. If they were in good physical condition, they exchanged their 12,000- to 16,000-foot residence for one hardly 2,000 feet

above sea level. From a land that yielded bare subsistence, they went to an environment rich in pine-
apples, bananas, sweet melons, beef and dairy cattle, yucca, corn, and dozens of vegetables.

The jungle was strange and unknown to all the
people from the *altiplano.* In the *alto Beni,* fear of
the jungle caused them to place their thatched huts
with latticed walls close to each other. They had
never before seen a machete or an ax. In the *altiplano* they had used llama dung and small bushes
for fuel. At Santa Ana, hardwood trees several feet
in diameter and a hundred feet high are common-
place. Four men among the first colonists were
killed in felling them.

So the *campesinos* had to be educated to the perils
and risks of the jungle. The use of the machete and
ax had to be explained. The proper way of felling
trees had to be demonstrated. There are poisonous
snakes in the jungle—the coral and the bushmaster
in particular. The python, who strangles men as well
as children, is also common; and the jungle is the
home of the jaguar and the wild boar. Colonists
from the *altiplano* had to be educated in these matters too. The environment of Santa Ana had new
risks; but they were outweighed by the advantages.

While none of the settlers professed a desire to return to the *altiplano,* 10 percent of those who left did
return there. Some of the new settlers in the *alto*

Beni were agricultural workers, displaced by the collateral effects of a land reform program initiated by the Paz government in 1953. I visited the village of Ucurena, not far from Cochabamba, where the new agrarian measures were announced. There it was proclaimed that the hacienda owners would be paid for their land in government bonds and that the *campesinos* would in turn pay for the tracts they received under long-term contracts. Such was the intention. But those plans fell by the wayside. The final result was that the land was confiscated, the owners losing every hectare except perhaps in the case of twenty- to thirty-acre plots. The *campesinos* received title from the government free of charge.

As between *campesinos* only rough justice was done. Some leaders of these rural federations prospered by taking more land than the amount to which they were entitled. They became the new centers of power, displacing the old landlord. And, like the landlord, they too exploited the *campesinos,* for example by selling them ammunition for their newly acquired rifles and keeping them cleaned out of cash. Some *campesinos* got holdings too small for viable farming units; others received land that provided only a subsistence crop. And so resettlement of agricultural workers became urgent. In the lush days, Bolivia produced 40,000 tons of tin a year; in the 60's the production went down to 20,000 tons.

As these mines ran into difficulties, excess labor appeared. Resettlement of these workers also became imperative.

For these and other reasons Civic Action moved to open the jungle by extending roads, by clearing the land, by advertising its program for colonization, by supplying colonists with easy, long-term contracts for acquiring their new homes, and by furnishing expert advice on the new agricultural, medical and economic problems of the *alto Beni.*

Resettling people in the jungle poses ecological problems. Jungle soil may be rich but cutting down the jungle may interfere with the creation of humus. Furthermore, as newly exposed soil is washed, laterization of the soil may develop, as it did in Southeast Asia. For such reasons, settlers in Costa Rica's cleared jungles had to leave the land after a few years. The long-range utility of these Bolivian jungle lands, therefore, remains in question.

At Santa Ana, Civic Action built thatch-roofed homes with sanitary outhouses for each family. Civic Action furnished a water supply that was pure. They built a first-aid center, outdoor basketball courts, a soccer field, and a schoolhouse. They brought in seeds and plants and helped the *campesinos* to prepare the soil. They established nurseries where coffee plants, for example, could be obtained. They offered an agricultural extension service to help the farmer through those difficulties solvable by pesticides, fertilizers and parasites.

Though Santa Ana is only 140 miles by road from La Paz, it is still remote. The road—perhaps the most picturesque in the world—is mostly one-way, with occasional turnouts for passing cars. A vehicle in the outside lane travels inches from an abyss that drops a sheer thousand to two thousand feet. This highway crosses a 16,600-foot pass, and is treacherous in fog and in darkness. Accidents are common.

Yet the road—which requires ten hours to traverse—is the only link, apart from the airstrip, between the colonists of Santa Ana and the world. Farmers in the jungle, Civic Action says, must have cash; and the best way to get it is to send nuts, tropical fruits and vegetables to the La Paz market. Since the small farmer perhaps never could afford a truck, Civic Action introduced a marketing cooperative. Education of the colonists of Santa Ana as to what constitutes a cooperative and how it operates was necessary. The cooperative concept is historically foreign both to the *altiplano* and to the jungle. For, over the years no *campesino* trusted anyone else, not even another *campesino*.

Civic Action went extensively into the construction of rural schools, each including sanitary latrines, a pure-water well and pump, and an annex where the teacher lives.

Civic Action also went into water supply projects for some 100 communities. One of its most spectacular successes in the field was at Achacachi, a town of 6,000 people in the *altiplano,* about 60 miles from La Paz. This town was held by leftist elements that ousted the Bolivian army from its barracks and installed a militia of leftist loyalties. For some years Achacachi sat aloof in splendid squalor, defying the central government. Father Jake of the Maryknoll Order went there in 1958 and used his quiet influence in moderation of the extremists to the left. In April 1963, Civic Action got in touch with him and proposed that it move in, not to level machine guns at the populace, but to give them water. The town jeered at this ruse to bring back the Bolivian army under the pretense of a water supply project, but Father Jake reassured the people and Civic Action did not disappoint them. On a morning in April, two dozen trucks appeared, carrying soldiers to be sure, but water pipes as well. Civic Action went to work and in seventy-eight days connected 40 percent of all the houses with pure cold water. The project cost $30,000 and each homeowner had to pay his pro-rata share. In time impure water will never again plague Achacachi with tuberculosis and dysentery.

Civic Action, while important as a catalyst for resettlement, was the symbol of far-reaching changes at work in Bolivia. The UN sponsored a resettlement area southeast of Santa Cruz at Cotoca. Here 80 families had a grim time, partly because of the nature of the soil, partly because of the weather. The winds in this region rise to 50 knots and fill the air with sand. The sand settles on the tile roofs in Santa Cruz so thickly that the seeds of cactus sprout there, making the drab houses joyous with color when the cacti bloom. Cotoca is too heavy with sand for good agricultural results.

There are many "spontaneous" resettlements scattered along the valleys below the *altiplano* and in the jungle as well. These "spontaneous" resettlements are without guidance or direction. Whenever a road is built leading down from the *altiplano* or a jungle road is extended, colonists appear overnight and start clearing land. The road down from La Paz to Santa Ana is lined with evidence of these squatters, kilometer after kilometer. They fell the trees and cut out the brush, setting fire to the slashings. But the wood is green and slow to burn in this damp, lush area, so crops are planted—usually bananas, corn, or sugar cane—amidst the stumps and the downlogs; and they will be sown this way until over a period of years the soil reclaims the forest debris. Many of these farms lie on forty-five-degree slopes; and it is not at all unusual to find some at sixty degrees. Terracing is seldom used, with the result that erosion is severe. Working these steep, narrow strips with machinery would be out of the question. Working them with oxen—the conventional draft animal in Bolivia—is difficult enough. As one Bolivian expressed it, "If a colonist is to succeed here, he should have a wife who is small in stature with good lungs, powerful legs and quick, nimble fingers."

The homes of these colonists are precarious affairs pitched on steep hillsides—remote and isolated, though they look down on dirt highways that connect them with La Paz.

The "spontaneous" colonists in the lower regions have brighter prospects. Santa Cruz, the home of the most beautiful women in Bolivia, lies about 2,000 feet high in the eastern jungle and is a burgeoning city. Gulf Oil Corporation had drilled its wells nearby. Each drilling operation required new roads; and the bulldozers had no sooner passed, than the "colonists" appeared out of the blue.

In the jungle areas Civic Action is prompt in building schools, and the government provides teachers through the sixth grade. Santa Cruz is a market for farm products; and the influx of "colonists" into that lower area is so great that "boom towns" are appearing. Montero, reminiscent of an Oklahoma frontier town a century ago, is one of them. Doctors and dentists have moved in; retail stores offering a wide variety of goods are multiplying; schools through twelfth grade are established; and all conveniences of urban life are appearing.

More important are the opportunities for employment both on the new farms and in the new factories that have sprung up. Critical, also, is a modern Agricultural Experimental Station owned by the Bolivian government with technical advice from Alliance for Progress.

Point Four—an unsung hero of American foreign aid—is mainly responsible for opening to development the vast jungle west of Santa Cruz. In the late 1940's, North Americans first took soil samples to see what crops would flourish, what rotation schedules would be necessary, what grasses would grow in the area. They cleared land with United States machinery and established experimental farms. Bolivia had known corn for a long time; indeed, it was produced in vast quantities for *chicha,* the sourmash beer used by the Indians on ceremonial occasions. But the modern production of corn was as foreign to Bolivia as nuclear energy. Traditionally, it took twenty hours to produce a bushel of corn in Bolivia, contrasted with Iowa's three-minute record. Point Four started the *campesinos* toward new production goals, by introducing a new species, the Cuban Yellow, and by teaching crop rotation between corn and rice. In the Santa Cruz area, our Point Four experts found many of the grasses of west Texas and introduced beef cattle. They also brought in dairy cattle and introduced the *campesinos* to the mysteries of butterfat, to the process of pasteurization, and to the secrets of cheese-making. Cotton raising was demonstrated; and the great potential of sugar cane was discovered and advertised.

The influx into the Santa Cruz area was as contagious as our own westward movement in the 1840's. Thousands of families settled there on farms of twenty to twenty-five acres each. Thousands more, from the *altiplano* and the high valleys below it, moved in as laborers. Opportunities multiplied fast. Sugar cane took hold. Four sugar mills—two government-owned and two privately owned—were built. These mills required much labor and the *campesinos* responded. Each mill became a self-sufficient community: a modern home for each family, with a garden plot; a first-aid center; a hospital with nursing and medical care; and a shopping center. Among the smallest sugar mills is La Belgioa, built by three men, the Gasser brothers of Belgium. Their management was so astute and their methods so modern and economical, that their one plant has been producing one half of Bolivia's entire sugar production.

Near Santa Cruz, a small group of Bolivians cleared 5,000 acres and planted cotton. They built cotton gins and finally a textile mill. Now they operate under the name of Algodonera, employing many hundreds of *campesinos*. In 1963 a new slaughtering plant for hogs was built in Santa Cruz.

Bolivia became self-sufficient in rice and sugar in 1963, but it is still deficient in wheat, edible oils, and cooking fats. Santa Cruz is not wheat country; but its prospects for lard and edible oils are bright, and the area will, before long, provide Bolivia with three million dollars a year in foreign exchange.

The agricultural well-being of the new jungle lands turns largely on the Agricultural Experimental Farm. The Farm was organized by Bolivian scientists, and Alliance for Progress experts gave technical advice. It is now racing to check the sugar cane borer that takes up to 50 percent of the sugar content of the cane. A search for parasites is on; and a concerted effort is being made to find a borer-resistant species.

Santa Cruz is breeding good beef cattle. The Church of the Brethren introduced the Heifer Club. Good stock was imported and presented to teenage farmers who promised to give their first heifer to a neighbor, who in turn did likewise, ad infinitum. Pigs, sheep, and chickens were added to the list of gift livestock, with the result that the circle of blue-blood ownership is ever widening. Our Four-H Clubs became Four-S Clubs—*saber* (to be knowledgeable), *sentir* (to have feelings), *servir* (to be willing to serve), *ser* (to express your individuality). They were particularly promoted by the Methodist Missions. Our Alliance for Progress experts became county agents, working long hours with the illiterate *campesinos* to make their small tracts richer by the year.

The *campesinos* were not in Santa Cruz long before they showed signs of a rising standard of living —bicycles and transistor radio sets. Their fields produce crops the year round; their cattle and hogs are fat; their chickens are good layers. The bloom of prosperity that the *altiplano* never knew is on the land.

This new mobility of the Indian population is probably the secret of the dynamism of Bolivia's revolution. They are a land-hungry peasantry conquering their frontier. The Indian, long held to one piece of land by serfdom, is now free to seek new horizons, new opportunities. And he is taking advantage of that freedom to improve his lot. This is a contagious influence. In some Latin American countries, the *campesinos* move out of the mountains to form slums around the large cities. In Bolivia that does not happen. There, many of the *campesinos* are on the move to build sparkling new farms along a frontier never exploited until the 1952 Revolution.

Bolivia, lowest in standard of living of all Latin American countries except Haiti, has a mean per capita income of about $105. The *campesinos* who have remained on the *altiplano* above Cochabamba have less than that, despite the attempts of Alliance for Progress and Civic Action to help. Eggs, cheese, milk, and vegetables are practically unknown to them. Potatoes, barley, and *quinoa* are their staples, grown from the thin soil that is so dry that when November rains fail, hunger stalks the land. Each *campesino* has a few llamas and a few sheep. Children cannot go to the schools that Civic Action erects in the valley because they are needed for herding the animals by day. Unless the *campesinos* resettle onto jungle land or onto land in the higher valleys where irrigation water is available, not much can be done to improve their crops. Much, however, can be done to improve their stock.

There are three members of the *Augunido* family in the *altiplano*—llamas, alpacas, and vicuñas; and each is related to the camel. They have the camel's capacity to travel for a long time without water; and the llama has the camel's bad habit of spitting in the face of a stranger. The llama is used as a pack animal and, with the alpaca and vicuña, for wool. Llamas can carry up to eighty pounds, though a twenty-pound pack is customary. They are notorious for their light-footed step and the safety with which they transport delicate, fragile goods. The *campesinos* eat them, of course; but their primary utility apart from transport is the wool. The *campesinos* prefer the black llama because the women like black wool best for spinning and weaving. Marketwise the white llama yields a higher grade of wool. Our AID undertook to educate the *campesinos* to breed mostly the white variety and so increase the family's cash return. AID also showed the *campesinos* how to improve the quality of the wool of both vicuña and alpaca. They traveled with mobile demonstration units, showing how to grade wool, how to spray the animals for worms and other parasites, how to breed for texture and fineness.

These teachings did improve the status of the *campesinos* in the *altiplano,* but almost imperceptibly. The environment is harsh and the agricultural potential slim. Yet the *campesinos* who live on the hills overlooking Cochabamba refuse even to visit the city. They do become mesmerized by the lights at night; they do come partway down to barter barley, wool, or *quinoa* for tomatoes, yucca, apples, and especially corn for making their *chicha,* and for coca leaves which they chew. But they cling tenaciously to their ancestral lands.

The main deterrents to migration are in the attitudes of the womenfolk. Those who move from 13,000 feet above sea level to 2,000 feet have an "adaptation sickness" that is temporary and relatively unimportant. The fear of tuberculosis (to which the highlander seems peculiarly susceptible) is a deterrent. More important are the culture and customs of the Quechua and Aymara Indians who have made their communities in the *altiplano* closed societies. Pachamama, the Inca Earth Mother, reigns there even though the people observe Catholic rites. From birth to death, ancient Inca rituals obtain. Days of fiesta follow the development of the corn crop in a definite cycle. When *chicha*, the national drink, is made, a white flag flies from the adobe hut. Travelers then know the beverage is for sale and stop to spend a few bolivianos in leisurely conversation. Everyone, including children, drinks *chicha*. There is no alcoholism among these Indians since there is no taboo against drinking. *Chicha* is a ritualistic drink and anyone who does get drunk, whether Mother or Father, is not denounced; one spouse waits patiently at the side of the one who has succumbed to alcohol, to bring him back to normalcy.

Migration to the valleys opens partway the door on the closed Indian society. Spanish must be learned if one is to be a commercial, instead of a subsistence, farmer. The heavy woolen clothes of the *altiplano* must give way to cotton.

The Indian is of medium stature and inclined to be thickset, with a large trunk but small hands and feet. His face is hairless; the cheekbones are prominent, the nose aquiline, the eyes like almonds. His hair is coarse and black, apparently never balding. The men wear rough woolen trousers held up by drawstrings; the shirt too is of rough wool. Resting on their shoulders is a poncho made from a tightly woven blanket with a hole in the center for the head. A felt hat is worn on top of a close-fitting cap that has long earflaps. Open sandals whose soles these days are made from cast-off automobile tires are their usual footgear. The Andean never bathes and probably changes his clothes only a few times in a lifetime.

The women, who are more Asiatic in appearance than the men, nurse their children for about two years and during that time carry them in pouches on their backs. They usually go barefoot. Their skirts, usually black, red, orange, yellow, or green, are full-cut with numerous pleats and they reach halfway between knee and ankle. These homespun skirts are worn one over the other. The blouse is short-sleeved, collarless, and buttoned down the front. A large shawl that reaches from neck to heels is pinned in front.

Those who know Bolivia can identify an Indian's village by the color and style of his dress. Black predominates in places; in others red stripes; in still others, orange. The women of the *altiplano* usually wear a derby hat—brown, black, or blue—at a rakish angle. "Who thought that up?" I asked Dr. José Ortiz Bello, a graduate of the University of Chicago Law School, who was my interpreter. José laughed as he said, "They say a British merchant had a surplus of derbys and sold them for a song to the *campesinos*." I discovered as I traveled from that high plateau to the jungle that practically every village has its own distinctive hat for its womenfolk.

The colonists who come down to the lower valleys and the jungle must accommodate to the heat. The men easily shift to cotton clothes. But the women are more tenacious. While one or two skirts are peeled off the first day, the derby hat and the heavy woolen garments are surrendered reluctantly. It may be months before the female embraces cotton slacks, a cotton blouse and skirt, and a straw hat; and even so the dresses brought from the *altiplano* are still treasured, and brought out for festive occasions.

Those who come down from the *altiplano* are in time greatly changed by the dominant Spanish culture, by modern machines, and by the mobility which shatters their ancient world. In the *altiplano* they chew coca leaves with ashes of potatoes, the consumption being about two pounds of leaves every ten days. The cocaine that they absorb relieves pangs of hunger and transforms dull gray clouds to reddish ones. The abundance of the lower land fills their stomachs and the coca leaf habit tends to wear away. While they make beer from corn in the *altiplano,* in the lowlands they make it from yucca. For a few bolivianos they can now purchase sugar alcohol, which appears in great abundance as a result of the molasses of the sugar mills for which there is no market. But whatever the source of the *chicha* and whatever its proof, the *campesinos* either high in the *altiplano* or deep in the jungle, as I have said, first place it in a gourd, raise it to the sky, pour a goodly draught on the ground for Pachamama, and then drink it down. Pachamama may in time become only a meaningless symbol; but this god of the Incas governs the *campesinos* of the *altiplano* and, if they migrate, travels with them.

In Bolivia, every worker belongs to some union (*sindicato*). These are modest versions of trade unions as we know them. Collective bargaining is in its infancy. So is grievance machinery, an unremedied complaint of one worker often resulting in a quick and costly strike. The unions manage contributing insurance programs which, like our Blue Cross and White Cross, cover sickness and hospitalization. But they also cover a host of other risks—unemployment, old age, and death itself.

Factory labor makes a minimum of $1.50 a day, farm labor 80 cents. Tin miners make on the average $3.00 a day, which includes fringe benefits.

The *sindicatos* cover every field of activity. Goods are smuggled extensively into Bolivia, some of the prize articles being Chilean wine and American cigarettes. People work full time at smuggling; and smuggling, like other work, needs protection. So the smugglers have their *sindicato.*

"Why?" I asked.

"To keep the standards up," I was told on a patio under a full moon in Santa Cruz. "Think how fraudulent it would be," my friend added, "if a smuggler took this fine Chilean wine and watered it down." After a pause, during which he sampled the wine, he concluded, "This bottle costs 25 cents in Chile and, thanks to the smugglers, only 50 cents here. That is possible only with high-class people in the union."

Shoeshine boys have their unions. So do taxi drivers. But these unions—unlike the political *sindicatos* of the *campesinos*—are guilds that restrict the number of people in the business and fix the rates.

The *campesinos* are also organized; but their unions in the context of rural Bolivian life were political organizations, expressing the will of the MNR, the revolutionary party under Paz. These rural *sindicatos* were in a way formidable affairs. Convoys of armed *campesinos* move about on strategic occasions, not to engage in combat but to rally public opinion. Guns and dynamite are widely held in the rural areas.

"It's nice to have dynamite for a political rally," one *campesino* told me.

"Where do you get it?"

"Someone can always smuggle it out of a mine."

The widespread presence of guns leads to bizarre events. I visited Cliza, not far from Cochabamba, which for years had a running fight in the old-fashioned Kentucky meaning of the term with nearby Ucurena. It really was a fight between competing *campesino* leaders. There were killings and more killings in revenge. Cliza, a popular trading center, lost its market place to Punata, another town, as neither merchants nor customers enjoyed the raiding back and forth.

The communists are present in Bolivia; but how many and just who they are is difficult to know. The lines they follow are unorthodox by current Soviet standards. They try mainly to get into the universities and into the unions. Some are self-proclaimed Stalinists; some are Trotskyites; some prefer Mao. Some have infiltrated MNR; others stick with their own small party organization. At least two universities have had communist rectors. Bolivian universities follow the Latin American pattern and give control to the faculty and the students. The communists seek to penetrate through those two groups.

The unions, not yet sophisticated or mature in Bolivia, have been perhaps the chief target of the communists. Their power has been put on display many times, usually headed by the Bolivian Workers Central, the national union that is supreme in the labor field. Central has put on pro-Castro rallies.

In 1952 the government nationalized the three big tin mines and since then has operated them through its agency, COMIBOL. Once COMIBOL took over, the people on the payrolls increased. This feather-bedding, plus inefficient mining operations, made the cost of tin ore $1.40 a pound on the average, which is higher than the world price. At one mine a pound of tin cost $3.67 to produce. A 40-million-dollar loan from the Inter-American Development Bank, West Germany, and the United States was promoted back in 1961 to deal with the tin mines. COMIBOL began to move for technological reforms. However, a strike was declared at Catavi, a town of 40,000 without a blade of grass and with monotonous mud-brick row houses. Five thousand miners laid down their tools at Catavi. Every miner had a gun and ammunition, it is said; the town had enough rice to last four months; and rumors were that Czech and Cuban money would supply all that was needed. Would the other mines follow Catavi and also strike against COMIBOL? At first they did; and the Paz government was faced with a major crisis.

Troops were not called out; no attempt at force was made. But the Paz forces did go quietly to work on redressing the situation and in about two weeks had all the mines except Catavi reopened. This was done by quiet persuasion, by removal of communists from key positions, by gentle pressure through noncommunist miners. Catavi remained closed and the Sierra Maestra, the name of Castro's old Cuban stronghold, was adopted in Catavi as the symbol of Bolivian resistance. The communist-coined object of the resistance is "Yankee imperialism," as it was the technical advice from the United States and the

Inter-American Development Bank that showed Bolivia how her tin mines could be modernized and made to pay.

The military regime that succeeded Paz "broke" Catavi. The miners were disarmed and their leaders exiled. Bonuses were abolished, payrolls were scrubbed, incentives were introduced to tie pay directly to productivity. By 1969 COMIBOL was in the black; and the cost of producing a pound of tin was down to $1.35. The cost of a tin stabilization program was financial dependence on the United States, gained at reestablishing the army as *the* domestic power.

We have been up to our ears in Bolivian politics, using our tin stockpile, our passion for private investment, and our checkbook to play politics. Bolivia is easy prey, as she is a poor country and needs U.S. markets and U.S. capital. The truth is that we are too rightist-oriented, too conditioned by the philosophy of the late Joseph McCarthy, too fearful of the left to deal in an adult way with the explosive political problems of Latin America.

We, along with the British, stood across the path of nationalists who wanted a tin refinery for Bolivia. For that monopoly was desired by Anglo-American interests. In 1970, however, Bolivia finally acquired a small tin refinery, built by West Germans, and is at last on her way to becoming the beneficiary of the exploitation of her own mineral resources.

The Maryknoll Fathers in their quiet way have worked wonders in Bolivia at the level of credit reforms. Bank credit is available only for the rich. A savings account earns 11 percent a year, which means that the bank paying it must make huge returns. The banks do not service the *campesinos* or the factory workers. Those people have had only the loan shark. Loan sharking in Bolivia is probably a risky business. In any event the charges are high. Ten percent a week, or 520 percent a year, is not unheard of. One hundred or 200 percent is common. The business is a lively one, for families have emergencies when $50 for an operation and for medicines may be the difference between life and death.

Father Daniel McLellan originally brought the idea of credit unions to Lima, Peru. This was back in 1950 when he was a young priest located at Puno on Lake Titicaca.

"Did you import the credit union when you came to Puno?" I asked.

"I had never heard of it," he answered; and then he proceeded to tell me the evolution of the idea.

At Puno various foreign experts came—U.S., American European—to tell the Indian how to improve his agriculture. But when they left, the Indian was still helpless.

"If they said he needed fertilizer, what would he use for money to buy it? If they said he needed a new plow, how would he acquire it? If he needed different seeds, how could he purchase them?"

The Indian wanted to improve his lot; but to do so he needed credit and even the loan sharks were far removed from the rural *altiplano.* The idea plagued Father Daniel and he wrote to the States. Pretty soon the Credit Union National Association of Wisconsin sent him literature and from it he got a glimmering of an institution that would serve the Indian's needs.

Another Maryknoll Father, Joseph F. Michenfelder, spoke up to say, "In this part of the world no one has trusted anyone. Why should the Indian? He has been exploited and enslaved throughout history. The white man especially is not to be trusted by the Indian. His promises were always broken."

Father Daniel and Father Joseph therefore had great hurdles to overcome. A credit union means entrusting someone with one's funds; it means banding together with a central management; it means launching a joint venture among people who are jealously individualistic. Patiently and calmly Father Daniel went about the creation of a credit union at Puno. He became the Treasurer. The problem was to find a group that had some communal ties. In a city, all those working in a factory or mine might constitute such a group. But which elements in a rural area would know each other and, knowing, be willing to trust one another in a business venture? The parish turned out to be the answer. And so the first credit union was born.

Later—when the credit union had taken root in Peru—Father Daniel and Father Joseph came to Bolivia. The idea has flourished there and, in less than two years, nearly 100 credit unions were formed either at the parish or factory or other working-unit level. In Bolivia the average loan is from $15 to $20. The interest charge is one percent a month on unpaid balances. About 40 percent of the loans are made to repay usurers. The rest of the loans run the gamut from weddings, funerals, and travel, to car repair and home improvements.

In 1963 AID got behind the credit union movement in Latin America.

Though credit unions had not started in Latin America until 1960, by 1968 there were 4,600 of them, with 2 million depositors whose average savings were $65 per depositor. That is an astounding record when it is remembered that most of these depositors had no more than $100 cash income a year.

When it came to the needed credit reforms, why were the padres of Bolivia silent for so long? The Maryknoll Fathers are the pacesetters. In all the credit unions in Bolivia, in all the co-ops, there is only one Bolivian padre. American priests, Belgian priests, German priests, Canadian priests—all supply some of the new ideas for the salvation of the *campensinos* from the otherwise certain drift to the maelstrom.

In talking with Father Daniel and Father Joseph, I began to see the high Andean country in new perspectives. From time out of mind the story had been wolf eat wolf. The Incas came, conquered, and regimented. The Spanish did the same, though more cruelly. No one could be trusted; and lingering suspicion of one's neighbor became a festering influence over the centuries. Man's only safety was in the security and solidarity of his family. No outsider could be trusted. Yet the Maryknoll Fathers knew that if ever a democratic system was to take hold in the Andes, bases of mutual trust must be laid. The credit union is a start. Beyond it lie other forms of cooperative action.

The marketing cooperative is being developed in Bolivia. The cooperative marketing of rice was an outstanding success. Other cooperative ventures are needed and in time perhaps cooperative production that will make possible the common use of farm machinery.

That day is probably far distant. But I remember a bright morning on the side of Potosí, about 14,000 feet high, where a cooperative was working the tailings for tin. Of the 5,000 miners at Potosí about one half are in co-ops—most of the co-ops are family affairs. It was a *fiesta* day—the day when everyone goes to the cemetery to decorate the graves. The entire mountain was still except at this one spot. Four men and a woman worked the tailings. The woman sorted pebbles by hand, placing in a precious pile those that showed tracings of tin. One man sifted smaller stones in a sieve; another used a settling basin where the rocks heavy with tin went to the bottom. No word was spoken, no song was sung; the group worked in silence. It was harmony required of a democratic society. But to acquire it means years of work under regimes that instill confidence, not fear.

Bolivia is about 60 percent illiterate. The total population is four million; but not more than 200,000 are pure Spanish. The Indians are mainly the Quechuas and Aymaras. Each has a distinct language; and not many Quechuas or Aymaras speak Spanish. Spanish-speaking people need interpreters when they travel Indian territory. Havana and Moscow have daily Quechua language broadcasts; and Indians who have transistor sets listen. Here again the Maryknoll Fathers are out in front. At Penas in the *altiplano,* they are conducting a literacy program by radio. They speak Quechua and teach Spanish. At receiving centers, Maryknoll Fathers supervise the classes. Pencils and papers are handed out and the *campesinos* receive their instruction first by the radio and then by the teacher at hand. Bolivia has no television; and poor roads and difficult altitudes make the distribution of movie films a considerable problem. The Maryknoll Order longs for films teaching literacy. The visual method would speed up the educational process considerably. But the radio method, though slow, is making a dent—thousands of *campesinos* have learned Spanish over the radio.

"What do the *campesinos* have to read after becoming literate?" I asked.

The answer was always the same: "New literature will have to be found."

And when I pressed for a more definite answer, it usually came down to reliance upon Maryknoll literature.

"The *campesinos* who can read Spanish can read the *Communist Manifesto*," one padre told me. "We want them to have other alternatives."

Teachers have been woefully scarce, though the country has a dozen normal schools trying to supply the demand. The teachers turned out by these normal schools make about fifteen dollars a month. If they are in or near cities, they get other jobs to supplement their income. In Cochabamba one worked as an accountant in the afternoon and as a journalist at night and yet did not make much over fifty dollars a month. Teachers assigned to a rural school are less fortunate. They live in the room that is built into the schoolhouse by Civic Action; but their life is lonely and they long for the diversions of the city. Their jobs are not attractive in terms of monetary rewards or living conditions; and they make up an army of teachers far too thin in the ranks.

There is a dearth of skilled labor in Bolivia. It takes a long time to get any mechanical device repaired, even an automobile, not to mention an electric shaver. Tractor schools have been conducted at some centers for farm labor. A polytechnical training school went up at Paracaya, near Cochabamba, where mechanics and carpentery, as well as handicrafts, home economics, and ceramics are taught. It offers two-year courses for about 200 students. This school was built by ILO of United Nations, with some Alliance for Progress money. Belgian unions also contributed some machinery, which is run by an enterprising Swiss.

United Nations experts (some sixty in all), Israeli technicians, German and British engineers, and American businessmen are by their deeds also showing what technology can do to develop an ancient society. American cooperative experts are introducing new dimensions in the thinking of the *campesinos*. Our AID people have spent twelve hours a day in a jeep visiting far-flung farms to help the *campesinos* find within themselves the capacity to raise their own standard of living.

I left Bolivia with the feeling I had seen something noble and enduring, not for the elite but for the many. There are visible signs of the increased physical well-being of the *campesinos*. Not often did I see bellies bloated from hunger; not many beggars appeared; the miserable mendicants of Asia and the Middle East who bore scars of disease and debilitation were not much in evidence. Two indices showed the better distribution of food during a recent decade: (1) the average weight of the army inductee was ten pounds heavier than in 1953; (2) the 1963 inductee was one inch taller than in 1953. From top to bottom something new and fresh and vibrant was in the air. A people was on the move; a great renaissance was in the making; a sense of mission was everywhere. This message was on the lips of schoolchildren pledging allegiance to their country as the flag rises over their thatched schoolhouse. It was in the energy of the colonists, making their new homes. It was present in the normal schools and on the farms; it permeated the Agricultural Experimental Farm at Santa Cruz; lawyers, doctors, teachers, engineers—all are speaking of the new world unrolling before them.

This spirit evidences much more than nationalism, though it includes it; and in a way, nationalism is its driving force. Nationalism in the sense of pride in history, pride in ideals, pride in the 1952 revolution.

The 1952 revolution made the Bolivians passionate advocates both of reform and of independence from external influence in internal affairs.

It was this sense of nationalism that led in 1969 to the nationalization of Gulf Oil. Thousands of Bolivians marched in the Andean capital, La Paz, in a parade honoring "The Day of Dignity." *Newsweek* reported what a *campesino* with Indian blood replied to American criticism that nationalization of Gulf would hurt Bolivia: "Our people will survive. Our wheat will be small and black but it will be our wheat."

While the revolution conditioned Bolivia—the poorest of South American nations—to enter the twenty-first century, it did not solve all of the basic problems. First is the problem of the military. In 1964 the progressive and enlightened Paz was displaced by a coup that installed Barrientos; when Barrientos was killed in an accident, the military displaced his civilian successor, Siles, with Alfredo Ovando, and late in 1970 Ovando was displaced by General Juan José Torres.

The army in Bolivia, like other Latin American armies, had never been subservient for long to the civilian authority as is the case in Anglo-American tradition. Presidents and regimes came and went in rapid succession until the 1952 revolution. A high Bolivian army officer explained the phenomenon:

"One had to have a certain mystique to serve long in the army," he said. "From lieutenant to major the salary was meager. From major on up, money came within reach, as did outside contacts. But there were no wars in the offing, no challenging problems of defense. What is this military group expected to do? Sit on its hands?"

President Paz decided on a different course for Bolivia. The Bolivian army was disbanded; local militia were established; the protection of the country was entrusted to them and to the *campesinos* who were heavily armed. In time the army was restored, finally reaching a strength of 10,000. Its functions were greatly changed; some arsenals were still guarded by the militia. But the military tradition was strong; and Bolivia marches into the twenty-first century, completely revolutionized, but under the iron hand of the military.

Second, is the content and meaning of the drive for development.

Ivan Illich* has told the sad story of developed *versus* underdeveloped nations, whether the developer be a staid capitalist or a revolutionary Marxist. The idea is to remake the underdeveloped nations in the image of consumers of packaged goods from the machines of the "advanced" nations. There is competition as to whose packaged goods the *campesino* will consume. But the end product is the same—his

* *Saturday Review,* October 17, 1970.

dual goal in life is to consume as many material goods as possible and, if possible, join the ranks of the privileged few and become a member of the group which does the processing or manufacturing.

This is the contagion in Bolivia's air and a contagion felt throughout Latin America. GNP has become man's obsession. Thus far, prices tend to put manufactured articles out of reach, and the prospect of making the *campesino* a member of the elite of consumers and producers seems very dim. But if the blueprint succeeds, think of the pollution that will ensue. And if men end up merely filling their stomachs with goodies and their homes with gadgets, think how miserable and frustrated men will in time become!

Men cannot live on GNP alone, as Prebisch has said. Witness the problems in the communist world. Budapest workers in 1956 and Szcecin workers in 1970 had as one of their demands freedom of speech and of press. Bread and vodka are not enough. Without a Jefferson type of First Amendment the rulers in the communist world do *not* know what the people are thinking, and the people deposit in their credibility banks mounting doubts and increasing lack of confidence because they have no way of learning just what their rulers are doing.

How can spiritual ideals be brought into a developing program? We know how to invest money and to train pilots of fighter planes and men to man tanks. But where are the blueprints for training people in freedom, liberty, and equality?

In the third place is the problem of education. All Latin American countries spend over 20 percent of their national budgets on education. In Bolivia, more than a third of the budget is spent annually on education. Illich says that "Bolivia is well on the way to suicide by an overdose of schooling." All schooling in Latin America is tuned to "development," which means the creation of an environment and educating or tooling man to fit into that environment. It is an attempt to educate man for life in a technological society that in terms of one generation or even more may be a never-never society. I left Bolivia wondering if, by reason of education, the oncoming generation is not destined to know only frustration. I wondered if there was the inventive genius to turn the young Latin minds toward a society based on spiritual as well as technological values. Is man destined to be only a consumer of things he does not need?

What the future will bring forth in Latin America, no one knows. One course is the historic bloody class struggle epitomized by Cuba, where a new power system rose out of the ashes of the old. That is only one possible course.

Another course is indicated by the military regime in Brazil which under the strong hands of "law and order" ruthlessly suppresses human rights and opts exclusively for economic gains.

A third course is a nationalistic and state-oriented Mexico. Inspired by like objectives, the Peruvian example may move in the same direction and develop along a similar course.

There is a fourth represented by Allende and the new government of Chile. This regime is more social-minded than any of the others and aims also for economic gains. It is profoundly revolutionary in the sense of identifying itself with the basic interest of the masses who represent the bottom of the pyramid. Perhaps the most telltale sign of its character is the presence in its ministry or senior staff of several highly competent, technically trained men drawn from ECLA. This group, with its primary emphasis upon the human values in the Chilean society, aims for accommodation rather than liquidation. In the minds of the intelligentsia, who have long worked for a restructuring of Latin American society, Chile will hopefully be the pattern on which future changes will take place in other Latin nations, and become indeed the bellwether of reform and revolution south of the Rio Grande. *Si Dios Quiere.*

VII

The Shadow of U.S. Industry over Latin America

The shadow of U.S. industrial grants over Latin America.

Primary production *versus* accelerated internal industrialization.

The history of U.S. direct investment in Latin America.

The terms of trade: exchanging commodities for manufactures.

U.S. capital benefits almost entirely the elite.

Capital accumulation is a prerequisite to industrialization.

The paradox of increased aid *versus* the debt explosion.

The United States casts even a darker shadow over Latin America than has been already suggested. Historically, Latin America has produced commodities for world trade, either agricultural or mineral; and these raw materials, not yet processed, bring a low price. With the foreign exchange from the sale of raw materials, imported goods are purchased; but their price is high. The industrialized nation benefits, for it needs raw materials for its factories; and it also needs markets for its manufactured goods. But the developing nation gets very little for its resources.

This adverse trend in the price of raw materials relative to the cost of manufactured goods (the terms of trade) manifests itself dramatically over the medium and long run: over periods of five to ten years or more. But in the short run, the price of raw materials faces another problem, namely oscillations from the trend. So, annually or over decades, the odds are weighted against the primary producing countries of the Third World.

The industrial pattern of Latin America shows generally the movement of raw materials to the ports and from thence to Europe and America. The local economy benefits from wages; but the profits and capital gains go abroad. While there are exceptions, this is the general pattern. Moreover, Western trading houses have poured Western goods into developing countries. This led in the old days to the destruction of local handicrafts in India and China. The same thing has been happening in Latin America where local handicrafts also have been destroyed by new industry. When industrialization takes over earlier artisan activities, the net effect is not employment, but unemployment. In Latin America, as in colonial Asia, the capital that might have been accumulated by local manufacturers and traders was often represented by the new foreign investments.

This product of the colonial period has been one consequence of the new imperialism of capitalistic regimes. It has helped negate the development of local industry and local markets in the developing nations, making them suppliers of raw materials for the industrial plants of the rich and making them also consumers of the products of the existing machines of mass production. The extent and depth of this development can be understood if it is remembered that Japan—the only Asian country free of colonial rule or intervention—was the first Asian nation to make an industrial breakthrough.

The reliance on primary products for export is stated by the Pearson Report to the UN:*

	Percent of Export Earnings, 1965
Tropical foodstuffs (sugar, coffee, cocoa, bananas)	21
Temperate zone food and fiber (cotton, meat, cereals, and wool)	16
Petroleum	26

* *Partners in Development,* p. 242.

Other mineral products (copper, iron ore,
    lead, zinc, tin)   11
Other primary products   10
Nonprimary products   16

Petroleum, coffee, and copper accounted for nearly half of Latin American export earnings in 1965. Half of the countries depend on a single product for more than half of export receipts (*e.g.*, oil in Venezuela, copper in Chile, coffee in Colombia, bananas in Ecuador), although there has been some progress in diversifying exports.

Yet the restraints on those exports have been damaging:

Few economic policies are as harmful to Latin American growth hopes as those which single out new and promising Latin American exports for restrictions in the United States market. Recent examples include limitations on United States import of Latin American meat, textiles, tomatoes, strawberries, and soluble coffee. European discrimination against Latin American exports, high domestic taxes on certain primary products, and "sanitary" controls also frustrate the achievement of higher export growth rates. *

The problem of Latin America starts with the fear that it may become the drawer of water and the hewer of wood for industry in the rich nations. That was the nub of the 1948 crisis between Yugoslavia

* *Partners in Development*, p. 257.

[121]

and the Soviet Union which led to a break in relations. For the Yugoslavs wanted a higher standard of living than was possible if they merely supplied the raw materials for the Soviet industrial plant and were the consumers of its products.

Dr. Richard N. Adams has stated:*

> Latin America has, for over a hundred years, been the mercantile hinterland of the industrial west. Since the Second World War, the United States has been its biggest buyer of raw materials and agricultural export crops and the largest supplier of imported goods. Within Latin America, a dualistic society provides the basically cheap labor that is a requisite to keeping prices on export items low. The U.S. housewife pays under a dollar for a pound of coffee; this means that the Latin American laborer working in coffee gets around 50 cents a day. Nowhere in the western world will 50 cents a day go very far. Yet the United States operates within a system that helps keep these wages at that level. There is no getting around this simple relationship, and no amount of diplomatic good will can alter the basic structural relationship that keeps Latin America in a subordinate position within the worldwide economic and power systems.

The fact that the United States is capitalist and Russia communist makes no difference at this level. Each has industrial machines that are hungry for raw materials. What percentage of the raw materials

* *Survey of Alliance for Progress*, Subcommittee on American Republics Affairs, U.S. Senate Foreign Relations, (1968), p. 208.

used in the industrial machines of the developed nations comes from outside those countries is difficult to determine.

The trend in the United States has been upward. Our total imports for manufacturing purposes were $5,201 million in 1960 and $6,300 million in 1967.

The wasting nature of mineral deposits, the declining grades of ore at home and the increasing competition for high-grade deposits abroad are the concern of our experts. In 1950 we had 9.5 percent of the world's population and we consumed about half of the world's minerals. At that time there was a 9 percent domestic production deficit. By 1970 that deficit was 20 percent and still widening. As to certain minerals, we are virtually dependent upon the foreign supply. Most of the material used in the manufacture of our military jet airplanes is imported. We import 99 percent of our platinum and chrome, 95 percent of our manganese, 72 percent of our tungsten, 100 percent of our tin and our industrial diamonds, 80 percent of our cobalt, 66 percent of our mercury, and 70 percent of our bauxite.

To cope with this problem, three main trends are discernible. First, the development of technology that will make profitable the processing of deposits, now marginal. Second, the search for alliances and trade agreements that will produce the needed minerals. Third, the tendency to make as our targets the development of operations overseas. And the latter

—whether American, English, French, Czech, Japanese, or Soviet—is obviously a form of imperialism.

Speaking of Japan, she is the modern exploiter of the unorganized, low-priced labor supply in Asia— first in Taiwan, then in Korea, finally in Southeast Asia.

American capital is in Latin America in considerable force. It produces benefits to the local government, *viz.* the present elite; and it provides some work for the people underneath. But the profits mostly go abroad; and our overseas plants, to a large degree, are devices to obtain commodities to keep our own industrial plants operating.

These factors, plus the intense nationalism in Latin America and the reality that a U.S. plant is a living symbol of our unpopular image, make for a trend to confiscate or appropriate U.S. industries south of the Rio Grande.

Apart from Cuba, there were in the last decade the following expropriations:

1960—Mexico's taking of a subsidiary of American and Foreign Power Company.

1961—Argentina's taking of all properties of American and Foreign Power Company.

1962—Colombia's expropriation of a subsidiary of American and Foreign Power Company.

1962—Brazil's taking of a firm owned by International Telephone and Telegraph Company.

1963—Brazil's taking of a subsidiary of American and Foreign Power Company.

1965—Chile's expropriation of a subsidiary of American and Foreign Power Company.

1967—Chile's expropriation of a majority in a Kennecott Company copper mine.

1968—Peru's taking over International Petroleum Company, owned by Standard Oil Company.

1969—Bolivia's taking of Gulf Oil Company; Peru's taking of a subsidiary of International Telephone and Telegraph Company; Chile's taking of a majority interest in an Anaconda Copper Company mine.

1970—To these figures must now be added the $964 million privately invested in Chile.

It is estimated that the properties taken total $3 billion. Still, $12 billion of U.S. business investments remain in Latin America.

When Franklin D. Roosevelt visited Brazil in 1936, he learned that the bus lines in Rio were owned by interests in Montreal and Toronto. On returning home, FDR asked, "What would the people of New York City do if the subways were all owned in Canada? Why, there would be a revolution."

The Council for Latin America in a recent report* emphasizes how U.S. private investments have

* Herbert K. May, *The Contributions of U.S. Private Investment to Latin America's Growth,* Council for Latin America, 1970.

promoted industrialization of the area, provided wages for workers and tax revenues to governments, and furthered the cause of developing managerial and technical skills. This is doubtless true.

The *net* contribution of U.S. private investment to Latin America's balance of payments during the period 1965 to 1968 was about $8.35 billion annually.

Of the total Latin American exports in 1966, the exports of U.S. affiliates represented about 35 percent.

Of the total Latin American exports of manufactured products in 1966, the exports of U.S. affiliates represented about 41 percent. Annual exports of manufactured products by U.S. affiliates increased by $585 million between 1957 and 1966, while such exports by all other producers combined increased by only $319 million or 51 percent.

The import needs of Latin America were reduced between 1965 and 1968 by about $8,070 million of commodities produced and sold by U.S. affiliates within Latin America.

The average rate of return on all U.S. private investments in Latin America was about 12.7 percent from 1960 to 1968, the return on U.S. manufacturing investments alone being about 10.4 percent. This rate of return was lower than the average rate of return on U.S. manufacturing investments anywhere else in the world, except in Canada.

Overall, U.S. private interests invested between

1965 and 1968 an average of $700 million a year and . earned an average of $1.44 billion a year, the net contribution to Latin America's balance of payments, as already mentioned, being $8.35 billion annually.

This honest account puts the best possible face on U.S. imperialism in Latin America.

Yet whatever may be said regarding the merits of a particular U.S. enterprise in Latin America and its contribution to "development," in the long run foreign private investment does not fit the long-term needs of any nation. Nationalism, the most rampant force south of the Rio Grande, will demand that the state itself or its nationals own the utilities and other corporations that are engaged in exploiting the local resources. Recent Peruvian experience is illustrative.

The Hickenlooper Amendment, 22 U.S.C. 2370(e)(1), provides that the President of the United States "shall suspend assistance" to a foreign government which (a) expropriates or nationalizes the property of an American corporation, and (b) fails in not more than six months to take steps to recompense "full value" for the property "in convertible foreign exchange." This Amendment came sharply into focus when the Peruvian military government took over the International Petroleum Company (IPC), a subsidiary of Standard Oil.*

* The entire story is told by Richard Goodwin in the May 17, 1969, issue of *The New Yorker*.

It is clear that the very existence of the Hicken-looper Amendment strengthened the resolve of IPC to fight to a bitter end and raised in the minds of Peruvians the specter of the United States in the role of the oppressor against a small and impoverished nation.

Peru, a nation of 12 million, has a per capita income of $280 and a GNP of $4 billion, while Standard Oil, owner of IPC, grows more than $14 billion a year.

The basic issue involved a question concerning ownership of subsoil rights. Generally in Latin America no private person can own the subsoil rights in land. They are owned by the state; an individual or corporation merely acquires rights to explore and exploit.

IPC claimed an exception because of a deed granted by Peru in 1826 to a private person, from whom IPC's title stemmed. Peru contested the merits of that claim and asserted that it need not pay IPC compensation for the property taken, since it was owned by the Peruvian government in the first place, and since IPC, indeed, owed Peru vast sums which it had received from exploiting Peru's property.

At long last IPC abandoned its claim of ownership; but by then the controversy was heated and out of bounds. The United States, for two years prior to the takeover, put the screws on Peru, not by invoking the Hickenlooper Amendment, but by finding excuses for withholding practically all aid to Peru. Though the Hickenlooper Amendment was not invoked, our State Department became solidly identified with the interests of IPC, and not with the development in Peru of a democratic, literate, prosperous nation.

This led to dire consequences when the Peruvian army seized IPC on December 4, 1968. The Peruvian General in charge said: "No people can live in dignity and with respect for its sovereignty when it tolerates the insolent arrogance of another state within its frontiers."

In spite of the record of expropriation, foreign investment in Latin America is not at a standstill. In December 1969, Peru entered into an agreement with an American consortium for a long-range project to develop copper deposits near the Chilean border. The enterprise was to include a railroad, power transmission lines, a water supply system, housing for mine workers, and a refinery on the sea coast. The investment was estimated at $355 million.

Private investment by foreign interests is one of the mainstays of the Rockefeller Report. The report gives the mistaken view that private investment by foreign interests in Latin America plays a key role in development. Yet, in some areas, it has proved wholly inexcusable and quite inflammatory. The tobacco industry in the Argentine was wholly developed by local people who then were bought out by British and American interests. The excuse that the outsiders were introducing new technology is nonsense. They were exploiters in the sense that they were gleaning profits from an underdeveloped nation for overseas use, not for local reinvestment. At present about 12 percent of the U.S. private investment in Latin America is in "trade," 6 percent in "public utilities," 32 percent in "manufacturing," 9 percent in "other." It is highly doubtful if these activities involve mysteries of technology not available to the Latins. The balance of U.S. private investment is 12 percent in "mining and smelting" and 29 percent in "petroleum." We North Americans may be more competent than most Latins to launch and manage these enterprises. If there are specialized areas where only very sophisticated men can manage successfully, then a case for partnership can be made attractive. But as an Argentinian of distinction asked me, "How can we have a true partnership when one is weak and impoverished and the other is rich and domineering?"

The answer is that outside private capital has a circumscribed role to play in the future of developing nations.

The future seems bleak for Latin America if the main reliance is on commodity trade. The powerful desire to industrialize quickly stems from the desire to obtain foreign exchange from exports of manufactured products. The value of world exports of manufactured articles increased at the rate of 8.1 percent annually from 1955 to 1968 as compared with a rate of 3.1 percent for commodities, or some two and a half times faster than the rate of increase of commodity imports. Trade in manufactured goods appears, therefore, to be the way in which to obtain rapid increases in export goods and foreign exchange.

Latin America has had little share in the expansion of world trade. Thus from 1955 to 1968, while merchandise exports from developed nations increased on a compound annual basis by 8.1 percent, exports from Latin American countries on the same basis rose by only 3.6 percent. In consequence, Latin America's share of world trade fell from 8.9 percent in 1955 to 5.7 percent in 1968 (trade of socialist countries excluded).

To repeat, while the price index of exports from developed areas to Latin America during the same period rose from 100 to 106 points, the price index of exports from Latin America to developed nations declined during that period from 100 to 96 points. The terms of trade (that is, the export price index divided by the import price index of Latin American countries to developed nations) declined consequentially from 100 to 91.

The composition of exports of Latin American countries shows the preponderance of primary commodities—food, agricultural raw materials, tobacco, beverages, mineral oil and fuel. Although manufactures including refined ores have been the most dynamic element of world exports, they accounted in 1967 for only 14.8 percent of the exports of Latin American countries.

The Atlantic countries take 60 percent of the manufactured exports from developing nations, the United States buying the most. But the total of these manufactured exports is less than 4 percent of the imports of the developed nations. The exports of manufactured goods by Latin American countries constituted in 1967 only about 21.3 percent of all developing countries' exports of manufactures and only about 1.7 percent of world exports of manufactured goods. Yet the Latin American nations bought nearly 23 percent of the manufactured products entering world trade in 1967.

The total manufactured exports from Latin American countries represented only about 14.8 percent of their total exports and 0.9 percent of world exports in 1967. The manufactured export trade is highly specialized and primarily concentrated on light products with a high labor content or on the processing of domestic raw materials. Moreover, manufacturing in Latin America is highly concentrated in food processing, metallurgy, textiles and other apparel items, and chemical products. About 61 percent of the total exports of Latin

American countries (all goods, including manufactures) originated in the following Latin American nations: Venezuela (24 percent), Brazil (16 percent), Argentina (11 percent), and Mexico (10 percent).

Because world trade in manufactured products has grown rapidly and promises to maintain that trend, the less developed countries, including Latin America, tend to regard industrialization as the quickest route to development; but stiff resistance to such an approach is maintained by high tariff walls and other restrictive trade policies of the developed countries.

The story is the same the world over. The eruption of violence in Ceylon in 1971 was due to the fact that because of lower world market prices, her export earnings from tea, rubber, and coconut declined while the cost of manufactured goods rose. The remedy through industrial diversification takes time and capital.

In any event, it appears that at present only a few of the less developed countries are capable of turning more and more to manufactures to increase export earnings; the rest must continue to rely on developing increased commodity exports, at least for some years to come.

This reliance on commodity exports for the creation of foreign exchange may be as dangerous to coffee nations, tea nations, and cocoa nations as it has been to rubber nations. Synthetic rubber had a profound impact on Southeast Asia. Gunnar Myrdal reported in 1965 that a synthetic coffee substitute will soon be marketed*, and that the laboratories of the world may push tea and cocoa as well "into the danger zone" where synthetics compete.

While the increase in manufactured exports from Latin America has been considered the true touchstone of economic development south of the Rio Grande, that increase may be of great importance to us as well. Late in 1969 David Rockefeller, in addressing himself to U.S.–Latin American relations, put the need of this country for Latin American imports in terms of helping to "discipline the immensely complicated cost structures of our economy." That is one aspect of the bilateral nature of the economic well-being of the countries of the world.

The economic plight of Latin America is extremely severe. Those nations with oil resources can, theoretically at least, convert them into factories, public housing, hospitals, schools, and the like. Most of them, however, are impoverished, having few natural resources except soil and people. The soil has not yet been opened up to scientific farming; the industrial plants are infants; and the people are not yet trained to the new tasks. This development of Latin America requires both capital and technical help. If the developing countries are to re-

* *Journal of Farm Economics,* No. 4.

ceive these kinds of aid in regular and sufficient amounts to transform their societies, the industrialized nations must establish somewhat the kind of relationship with them that they have with the poverty areas within their own boundaries.

For industrialization to proceed successfully, capital accumulation is the first problem, whether it be private capitalism or state capitalism.

Capital accumulation plus technological competence are, in this age, hardly enough, however, to produce a viable society. Today's problem is to build an industrial system on a broad popular base, not to create an exploitive industrial oligarchy.

Former Ambassador Covey T. Oliver, who served us in Colombia, said: ". . . economic development with only incidental social betterment components is no more than 'trickle down,' a philosophy of peaceful revolution that has never worked anywhere in the developed world. All the more reason why it should not be expected to work in the far weaker distributive structures of the developing countries."

The capital furnished through Alliance for Progress and other U.S. sources has not, however, resulted in a revolutionary industrialism embracing a whole people and extending its dynamism to the entire economy. It has not been geared to the needs of the masses.

The capital advances we have made have exacted a heavy price. The funds have, in large part, been committed for expenditure in the United States. That procurement provision *plus* amortization, plus interest payments, has meant that out of every five dollars advanced we got four dollars back. The aid has cost us little indeed.

President Nixon ordered that, as of November 1, 1969, "loan dollars sent to Latin America under AID be freed to allow purchase not only here, but anywhere in Latin America." From that time on recipients of U.S aid could spend their AID dollars, shopping for a better price than the U.S. monopoly offered—yet they still are barred from shopping in Europe or Asia.

There are those who think we may reach the point with some nations where the inflow of capital into the developing country will balance the services on the old debt. That is what David Horowitz of Israel called "a peak of respectability" by financial standards and "a peak of futility" so far as the problems of the developing nations are concerned.

The debt-service ratio (interest and amortization on external debts over proceeds from exports of goods and services) has mounted sharply in developing countries. Mexico has maintained a debt-service ratio of about 39 percent without default or need for debt rescheduling. Most other countries are not as fortunate. The Argentine, with a debt-service ratio of 25.3 percent (1966), and Brazil, 30.6 percent (1966), seem headed for trouble.

There are those who maintain that capitalism generated and maintained underdevelopment in Latin America.* Whatever may be the validity of that thesis, historically speaking, it now seems pretty clear that capitalism and the bourgois mentality in Latin America are incapable of leading Latin America out of the underdevelopment which paralyzes it.

The bourgeois mentality is geared only to servicing the elite, not to the vast restructuring of Latin American society that is needed if the masses, as well as the elite, are to be admitted to first class, participating citizenship. Unhappily, the United States is the mainstay of the bourgeois mentality. Yet ideas are too potent for any bloc to control. Out of the bourgeoisie will come a nucleus of 5 percent or 10 percent who will mold the revolutionary program that will remake Latin America.

* Andrew G. Frank, *Capitalism and Underdevelopment in Latin America*, Monthly Review Press, 1967.

VIII

Misconceptions of Latin American Folklore

Our folklore and theirs involve seven conceptual problems:

(1) participatory democracy

(2) private enterprise

(3) the family farm

(4) conservation needs

(5) surplus labor

(6) the Reformation, and

(7) population, technology, and the farm-to-city drift

The danger of introducing labor-expelling technology

The Japanese illustration

The problems of Latin America are in some aspects unique.

First, there is a contradiction between the existing power structure and the feasibility of creating new structural forms that reach the majority of the population. Economic measures are not enough. Social change in Latin America is dependent on changes in the political institutions, which means not a liquidation of the elite but a revolution in the Mexican and Bolivian sense of the word, and a real subservience of the military.

Second, private enterprise has not been the dynamic force it has been in the United States. The rich middle class of Latin America did not make its money by invention, by building plants, by merchandising. It discovered its wealth—gold, silver, tin; and became rich by owning land. In business, it specialized mostly in exports and imports; and the aura of insecurity surrounding the system led the middle class to export its capital to depositories in the United States and Europe. There is indeed a basis for the belief that U.S. aid made it possible for the elite to liquidate many of its holdings in Latin America for deposit and safekeeping overseas.

Third, the elite of Latin America appropriated all the available agricultural land before the great European immigrations of the late nineteenth and twentieth centuries. Argentina and Uruguay are conspicuous examples. The new arrivals faced the prospect of being tenant farmers or rural workers. For those below the elite, no units of family-owned property were available. No species of democracy therefore developed at the grass roots. Where the hacienda system prevailed, there was feudalism and paternalism, but no semblance of democracy.

The Alliance for Progress represented a new version of an old American fable: that the triple formula of private enterprise, grass-roots democracy, and the family farm will make every people happy. But those aims—no matter how worthy—can be realized only if they become a part of Latin American politics. Expectations of changes by reason of fast infusions of money from the United States are only wishful thinking.

Jeffersonian political philosophy gave the United States a freeholder's land tenure system and resulted in an agrarian middle class. Congress, with strong rural representation, appropriated funds for the needs of the countryside. By the time our frontier closed we had a backlog of well-developed state and local governments, a compulsory school system, an active extension service, widespread literacy, and well-established communications networks, including rural free delivery. And some think that many of these, including a compulsory school system, are anachronistic to the needs of Latin America.

However that may be, these conditions—which by our folklore are the norm—simply do not exist in

Latin America. There, the dominant pattern, symbolized by the hacienda system, is concentration of agricultural lands in the hands of a few. Between 5 and 10 percent of the landowners in Latin America control between 70 and 90 percent of the agricultural lands. Yet nearly 50 percent of the work force in Latin America is engaged in agriculture. The introduction of technology in agriculture means, therefore, a great displacement of agricultural workers.

The concentration of agricultural land ownership in Latin America has had numerous other ramifications. When the yields per unit of land increased as a result of technical progress, the landowner received most of the benefits. There was no corresponding rise in the income of the masses working the land. Their pressure on the land increased; and the land, when broken up for distribution, was divided into ever smaller plots. The result in Latin America, as Dr. Prebisch shows, is that "peasants inherit a single furrow." Thus basic, far-reaching land reform becomes imperative.

Moreover, the concentration of land ownership has meant the impoverishment of local governments. Municipalities are expected to build and maintain roads, schools, hospitals, and public utilities, and to control marketing facilities. But the rights of the majority to assess and collect taxes and select their own local officials are defeated by the elite. As a result, no unit of government can respond to the requirements for the capital needed by rural communities. Revenues collected by rural municipalities come from commercial business licenses, fines and fees, departmental transfers, and some property taxes. Those who own most of the resources contribute little tax revenue. Thus the communities are afforded so few funds that by the time they pay local salaries and administrative costs there is nothing left to supply municipal services.

A low rate of taxation, a high delinquency rate in tax payment, and insufficient autonomy of the local governmental unit thwart local development. That this issue will be difficult to cope with is obvious—local governmental units are largely dominated by bosses, many of whom control most of the privately owned resources in the area and are able to manipulate municipal finances for patronage rather than developmental needs.

Fourth, Latin America has no real conservation movement. We who live north of the Rio Grande have about ruined the ecology of our nation by the rush to convert everything into dollars. Latin America has not reached that destructive level; but it is not laying many foundations on which an ecological approach to the earth and its wonders can be expected.

To some extent conservation is a hemispheric problem. The decimation of forests, soil erosion, water pollution and now air pollution, as well as disappearing species of wildlife, are mounting contemporary problems; and Latin America is decades away from facing them.

The man who carries a gun in Latin America shoots at everything that moves. In that respect he is like the American Indians, our early settlers, as well as the present unregenerate Texans. In Brazil they say, "Shoot it if it moves. If it doesn't move, paint it white." There is, however, one extenuating circumstance. Half of the people are below the subsistence level; and 30 percent have barely enough to live. It is therefore a temptation—at times a necessity—to take what one can get to keep the family alive.

Below the equator the flyways generally go south, not north. There are six shearwaters and three petrels that breed south of the equator and winter north of it. Two small birds—the forked-tailed flycatcher and a swallow—breed in Argentina and Paraguay and cross the equator and winter in Venezuela. Numerous North American birds regularly winter south of the equator—purple martins, chimney swifts, three swallows, a flycatcher, nighthawks, many shore birds, gulls, terns, and jaegers.

There are many national "parks" in Latin America. Chile, for example, has forty-three. But there is not yet much awareness of the ecological values which are involved. Parks are often thought of as a resource for the production of lumber, not as sanctuaries for wildlife, for rare trees such as the alerce (*Fitzroya cupressoides*), or even for man himself. It is common for squatters to settle in national parks; and there are not enough supervisors and rangers to oust them, let alone to patrol against damage caused by their axes and their fires. In Latin America, as in other developing countries, conservation receives a low priority. The sad fact is that by the time Latin America is developed, many of its natural wonders may have become extinct.

It is this gravity of the conservation problem and lack of governmental tools to deal with it that the Rockefeller Report emphasizes. Indeed, it recommends that OAS take the lead in the conservation movement.

Fifth, most of Latin America (Argentina, Chile, and Uruguay being exceptions) has enjoyed a great surplus of labor, provided not only by Indians but by imported Negro slaves. This has led to a great saturation of people at the subsistence level with no prospect of improvement.

No country has been exemplary when it comes to the treatment of its poor. In Latin America the attitude of the elite has always seemed especially callous. There are many exceptions, though the common assumption is that the miserable people at the bottom will get their reward "in Heaven," not on this earth. The historic utterance by the Archbishop of Lima about thirty years ago that exalted the status quo was as follows: "Poverty is the most certain road to eternal felicity. Only the state which succeeds in making the poor appreciate the spiritual treasures of poverty can solve its social problems." And so the class differences seem enormous, even to one who comes from a country full of class differences.

Sixth, Latin America missed the leavening effects of the Reformation. The Reformation of the sixteenth century did not in itself, of course, create nationalism. But it did provide an inquest on the Holy Roman Empire and gave a great fillip to nationalism even in its extreme manifestations. And the growth of nationalism was never sturdier than in Latin America. This, however, is not the point of the absence of a Reformation in Latin America. The point is that the Church in that region never experienced the cleansing effect of dissent and separatism and has remained authoritarian and deeply wedded to the status quo.

The Catholic Church had a monopoly and used its influence not to build cooperatives or health centers or deep-freezes for the masses, but to obtain gold for conversion into leaves which would decorate the walls of massive cathedrals. Not all prelates in Latin America are so benighted. The bishops of Chile are highly enlightened; and every country has priests with a more humanitarian view. But it took the priests from Europe and from the United States, rather than the Latin American clergy, to bring into being dynamic forces of social change. Of these the Maryknoll Fathers have been preeminent.

Seventh, the population explosion and the technological revolution in agriculture will have a profound effect in Latin America. Yet, as noted, the people are drifting to the cities looking for improved opportunities.

The five million destitutes who form a ring around Lima, Peru, live in shelters made of packing cases and pieces of sheet metal—no food, no amenities of life, no medical care—a great and growing social cancer. Quite similar conditions obtain in so-called prosperous and progressive Mexico City.

When the agricultural revolution in Latin America is complete, what will happen to the great excess of labor that will leave the farms? The problem is the same as the basic, competing ideology of Liu Shao-ch'i and Mao Tse-tung—the contest that Mao won in his emphasis upon village development.

Industry has been thought of as the absorbent of surplus labor. Industrialization of developing nations has been preached on all the continents as the salvation for underprivileged people. But, under the new technology, machines will more and more take the place of men. Service industries will absorb some of the displaced people. But we know that automation will place an increasing number of workers in the leisure class.

We already have bakeries without any bakers.
Elevator operators have all but disappeared.

In big industry the greatest progress toward disemployment has been made in the petrochemical industry.

John Snyder writes:*

. . . there is no question that automation is already a major cause of unemployment in this country, or that automated machines will essentially take many more jobs from men than they have already.

ITEM: At one plant, one man today operates one machine which performs more than 500 separate manufacturing functions that formerly took some 70 men to perform.

ITEM: In a similar plant, 48 men using automated equipment today turn out a finished product in 20 minutes. Before automation, it took 400 men 40 minutes to do the same job.

ITEM: In an electronics plant where 200 men used to assemble 1,000 units a day, only two men now turn out just as many with the help of automatic machines.

ITEM: A three-man crew in a "robot" steel mill turns out 217 miles of rod per day at more than twice the old rate and at one-tenth the old labor cost.

ITEM: A major Government agency, using computers, has cut its clerical work force from 13,000 to 3,000 workers.

* "Automation: Threat & Promise," *New York Times Magazine,* March 22, 1964.

Many argue, however, that as old jobs disappear, new ones are created. But automation, it is estimated, eliminates 40,000 jobs a week or more than two million a year. Thus at best the retraining of workers and their placement in new jobs in near or distant cities present a staggering problem. The introduction of work-free plants in Latin America would compound that problem.

The Lavelle Study in automation of 1961–1962, strongly endorsed by the United Steel Workers of America, shows (1) that production levels are being increased with a declining work force; (2) that full employment is no longer a prerequisite for increased production; and (3) that production output is rising even as the ranks of the unemployed are swelled. The answer of the United Steel Workers and other unions is a thirty-two-hour work week or four-day week.

The trend of industrial employment is down:*

Production Worker Employment Trends (U.S.)

1947–1960

INDUSTRY	EMPLOYMENT	
	1947–1953	*1953–1960*
All Manufacturing	up 8.1%	down 11.3%
Iron and Steel	up 4.4%	down 16.8%
Nonferrous Metals	up 4.6%	down 17.1%
Autos, Trucks, Parts	up 18.2%	down 20.2%

* Conference on Economic Progress, Jobs and Growth, Washington, D.C., May 1961.

Moreover, output is increasing as is unemployment; but so is idleness in plant capacity:*

PERCENT OF PLANT CAPACITY IDLE (U.S.)
(*McGraw-Hill Annual Surveys*)

INDUSTRY	1954–1960	Sept. 1960
	(ANNUAL AVERAGE)	
Iron and Steel	19.1%	48%
Nonelectrical Machinery	23.1%	28%
Electrical Machinery	16.3%	26%
Autos, Trucks, Parts	13.5%	14%
Other Transportation Equipment	26.4%	27%
Chemicals	18.3%	23%
Rubber	14.4%	15%
Petroleum Refining	10.3%	17%

The example of Japan is cited as disproving this thesis. Japan is a fast-developing technological society with a relatively small labor force. By custom and usage, labor has ties to plants and to communities which give it a large degree of protection against sudden displacement. But technology has had a great impact on labor, evidenced in part by the large amount of underemployment. Yet underemployment is a fact difficult to reduce to reliable statistical form; it apparently affects not younger workers so much as those above 35 years of age. Rapid technological changes in Japan, however, have stimulated

* *Ibid.*

[151]

investment in new industries. Moreover, increased employment and rising wages caused the demand for consumer goods to mount, and this in turn meant an expansion of industries producing those goods. The result has been an increase of one million wage earners each year.

Yet in at least two industries—coal mining and chemicals—there have been technological declines in employment which necessitated vast government planning. In Japan the degree of planning in the field of labor reaches dimensions we have never known, save in time of war.*

The Japanese experience holds little hope for Latin America. Latin labor is under no protective paternalistic regime comparable to Japan's. Moreover, Latin America's population in the 1960's was increasing at the galloping rate of 3 percent a year, while the rate of Japan's population increase is only 1 percent a year.

In the United States, computer-controlled manufacturing functions, industrial robots, and controlled lathes are emerging as new automated facilities. As much as 50 percent of today's labor force will shortly be displaced, and at least 80 percent will be displaced eventually. How many workers will have new job opportunities is conjectural. By the end of this century all major industries will be con-

* Labour Automation, Bull. No. 7, Manpower Adjustment Programmes: III Canada, Italy, Japan, I.L.O.,1968.

trolled by computers. Our factories will be largely workerless, run by machines. Oil companies are already discussing ways of running entire refineries by machines. Steel companies are replacing skilled draftsmen who mix high-quality metals to make alloys with accident-proof computers. Newspapers are being set electronically. Labor unions in this field face the cold reality of an exploding technology in the newspaper business that means an end to more and more labor.*

In Latin America there is a growing awareness of the problem. Indeed, a group of us were discussing it in Peru, where a new china industry, employing two hundred workers, was so completely modern that it turned out articles so fast that the employees were out of work for about nine months each year.

The Prebisch Report, *Change and Development, Latin America's Great Task* (July 1970), is the most challenging and penetrating on the socioeconomic plight of Latin America. He discusses "the clear-cut dilemma of the choice between productivity and employment" and concludes with these words: ". . . unless the rate of economic development is stepped up, the transfer of redundant manpower

* The other studies are Michael, *Cybernation: The Silent Conquest* (1962); Hetstein et al., *Jobs, Machines, and People* (1964); and Wilkinson et al., *Technology and Human Values* (1966)—all published by the Center for the Study of Democratic Institutions, Santa Barbara.

from rural to urban areas will continue, to say nothing of the unfavourable effect that relatively slow-growing domestic demand may have on agricultural prices."

The inability of industrialization to solve the unemployment problem is stated in the Pearson Report:* ". . . manufacturing employment for the whole of Latin America has grown less rapidly than the labor force, at a rate around 2 percent per annum, and manufacturing has absorbed less than 15 percent of the new workers. Urban unemployment and underemployment have become serious even in the rapidly growing countries."

What are the alternatives?

All the power available—military, financial, industrial—can be aligned to prop up the present system. This system, however, is so intolerable for 80 percent of the people that any such approval will generate a generalized Chinese-type revolution.

People in Latin America—the voiceless illiterates at the bottom of the pyramid—know that China has made great achievements. News travels fast these days; and the *campesinos* know that mass starvation, which plagued China for centuries, has disappeared. China's standard of living is low. But it is higher than that of the millions of people who ring Lima and Mexico City in miserable huts.

* *Partners in Development,* p. 243.

Edward K. Hamilton of the Brookings Institution commented:*

When we look at the income levels in China and those in some other underdeveloped countries, it seems to us that if we can bring the standard of living up to our own developed level in forty to a hundred years, we've made good progress. So, even if we can convince students that progress can be made without destroying everything first, the pattern we offer, our fits and starts, must seem to them an unsatisfying prospect. They tend to think in immediate terms. To the extent that the students force us to reexamine our ideas and to weigh our progress against our values and objectives, I think they are performing an enormously valuable service.

Dr. Prebisch said about youth on the Latin American left:**

The mere idea of a chaotic situation is attractive to the youth because they see Mao as trying to destroy the remnants of the old society. The prevailing idea, I would say, of the Latin American youth on the left is that society is so bad they must destroy it. They do not resent the chaotic situation that the Cultural Revolution has created in China. On the contrary, they admire it as a way of clearing the ground for better things to come.

* *One Spark from Holocaust: The Crisis in Latin America* (Symposium, Center for the Study of Democratic Institutions, Santa Barbara, California, 1970).
** *Ibid.*

The industrialized nations now have machines that can supply most of the earth with physical things that people need. Some people dream of tying Latin America into such a scheme, of trying to do there what Russia tried to do in 1948 in Yugoslavia. The resources of Latin America would then feed our industrial machine—or ours plus Europe's, Japan's, and Russia's. This would be theoretically possible, but in fact disastrous. It would be the incarnation of the new imperialism that Latin Americans already talk about. It would hasten the new revolution faster than trying to maintain the status quo. A third alternative is the only realistic one.

IX

The Need for a Wholly New Approach

(1) Multilateral action under the United Nations

(2) withdrawal of all military missions and military aid

(3) creation of a Pan-American satellite for educational purposes

(4) village renovation as nucleus for action especially as regards food production, population control, and land reform

(5) labor-intensive investment program

(6) the idea of a hemispheric co-op

A wholly new approach must be taken; and that entails a few preliminary matters.

First. Our assistance to developing nations is needed and it should continue; but it should be furnished via the available multilateral or United Nations agencies. The need for this change in policy is especially great in respect to Latin America. The granting of aid involves politics, and Latin Americans can see in U.S. loans real or fancied hobgoblins. Aid is a means of obtaining leverage over a nation and its policies. This is a greater source of discontent and complaint than any other single factor. Aid can be effective in promoting structural reforms in Latin America only if it is divorced from the United States and the suspicion of the people that it serves our interests primarily and their interests secondarily.

There are several intermediate positions. Some would place no restrictions on national loans or grants. The Rockefeller Report would limit multinational agencies to the financing of "the bulk of public works projects" and these loans would be restricted "to agriculture, education, public health, and urban development projects which involve pioneering and testing new approaches."

Those who favor the availability of national loans or grants, point to the hardship which would ensue if a developing nation were dependent solely on a multinational bank or fiscal agency with the result that it became caught in the bind of an international bureaucracy as oppressive as that of any government's own administrative arm. There is much to be said for that position; and, whatever one may think ideal, national interests will doubtless compete with multinational agencies to finance needy nations.

In any event, the Hickenlooper Amendment is obsolete. As already noted, it directs the President to suspend all U.S. aid to a nation which nationalizes, expropriates or seizes property owned by U.S. interests, or repudiates or nullifies existing contracts or agreements with U.S. interests, or imposes discriminatory taxes on them. American private interests might hesitate to go into a country without some kind of deterrent of that character. But the Rockefeller Report recommended that the Hickenlooper Amendment be suspended or modified. It should be discarded.

The Hickenlooper Amendment is only one of several leverages which we have designed to use against developing nations, including Latin America.

The Pell Act authorizes the withholding of aid to any nation that seizes a U.S. fishing vessel [79 Stat. 660]. The Conte-Long Act directs the President to withhold economic aid in an amount equivalent to the amount spent by a developing nation in purchasing "sophisticated weapons system" [82 Stat. 964, 1138]. The Symington Act directs the President to cut off aid to and trade with a developing nation whose resources are being diverted to "unnecessary military expenditures to a degree which materially interferes with its development" [81 Stat. 459]. The Reuss Act bars the Export-Import Bank from extending credit to a developing nation that expends in an arms race "scarce foreign exchange needed for peaceful economic progress" [82 Stat. 47, 48].

The Rockefeller Report suggested that these acts be modified or suspended.

Moreover, the Merchant Marine Act provides in general that at least 50 percent of the gross tonnage of articles of foreign aid be shipped in U.S. bottoms [46 U.S.C. 1241], apart from a few exceptions [22 U.S.C. 23–53].

The Rockefeller Report suggests that this provision be repealed.

So far as Latin America is concerned, it is impossible to justify any of these measures if we are to get onto a cooperative basis with all nations in this hemisphere.

Apart from training schools and technical laboratories, the blueprint of the future will in no event tolerate the presence of foreign-moneyed interests except on a partnership basis. The equality demanded for the future will tolerate neither exploitation of local resources by outside interests nor the long arm of outside control. So the era of aid as a lever on political action is near its end.

Second. The withdrawal of all of our military missions has peculiar relevance to Latin America. We are the procreators of dictatorships. Our Pentagon is ideologically tied to the elite of Latin America who need the military to keep in control. Our military presence in Latin America can only cause endless mischief and discord and separate this nation more and more from the aspirations of the people south of the Rio Grande.

Since 1961 the United States Arms Sales Program has been in an office of the Pentagon called International Logistics Negotiations (ILN). The Foreign Affairs Committee of the Senate has called ILN's approach to its task "dynamic and aggressive." ILN has emphasized in its sales efforts not only the military and the political point of view but the economic as well:

> From the economic point of view the stability of the dollar in the world market is dependent on our ability to resolve balance of payments problems. Failure to resolve these balance of payments problems creates economic pressures in the international and in the domestic spheres. The solution to balance of payments is principally in more trade. All other solutions merely temporize the problem.

So far as developing nations are concerned, military sales amount to only 12 percent of the total. This indicates, as the Foreign Relations Committee of the Senate has suggested, that economic considerations are not important in our arms program when areas such as Latin America are involved. There, the military sales are designed (1) to influence "the development of the local military elites" or (2) to achieve "preemptive selling," *viz.* "preventing the influx of military equipment of other nations."

But the U.S. sales campaign of arms has been so successful in Europe that our unsuccessful European competitors have turned to the Third World, including Latin America, and have succeeded in selling airplanes of a most sophisticated nature to these areas. These military sales are traditionally "hard money" sales that add to the debit-service problems of the purchasing nation. These payments compete with payments made on outside debts for modernization and industrialization. The two combined are responsible for two thirds of Latin America's foreign exchange deficit.

The annual expenditure of Latin American countries on armaments has reached $1.5 billion, while the average yearly sum advanced by the United States under the Alliance for Progress was $1.1 billion. How subversion can be deterred or stopped by fifty-ton tanks, supersonic aircraft, and battleships is a mystery.

Where are the external dangers which demand these sophisticated weapons? Prestige of one military clique in one nation suffers, of course, if the neighbor is armed with missiles and the like. But why waste the resources of nations on armaments when the ring of hungry people forming around the capitals in Latin America continues to grow?

This is a matter for the collective action of the nations of this hemisphere. It obviously cannot be solved unless the United States changes its military stance toward the world, including Latin America. For Latin America would never be content to remain armless, leaving her protection and salvation to her neighbor north of the Rio Grande.

As I have said, about 7 percent of Alliance for Progress aid went to military projects. President Johnson, in 1967, spoke of eliminating unnecessary military expenditures by Latin America. But again that was more words than substance. Under the Pentagon and the CIA, we went headlong into armament unmindful of the fact that the cost of one supersonic aircraft squadron can build and maintain many hospitals.

Third. We must create a Pan American TV satellite system and help in technical aspects to make it a powerful educational force at the village level.

The linguistic nexus with Latin America has presented serious problems. Few schools in the United States offer a four-year college course in Spanish and, so far as I am aware, none offers one in Portuguese. A Latin American coming here for an education must speak and write English. The sons and daughters of the top 20-percent elite are usually so trained; and they troop here for an education. Thus

1966 brought here the following numbers: the Caribbean, 991; Central America, 478; Mexico, 309; South America, 1,593. And for 1967 the following were the figures: the Caribbean, 1,396; Central America, 772; Mexico, 686; South America, 2,839.

But that flow from the families of the rich represents only a very small segment of Latin America. Our educational opportunities do not reach the overwhelming majority—the 80 percent, made up of Indians and *campesinos*. They are largely neglected at home, there being few schools for them. So by percentage, not many from the lower 80 percent qualify for the higher education we offer—even if somehow they obtain the magic scholarship.

I explored the problem through the Parvin Foundation, which had programs at Princeton and at UCLA for training future leaders in developing nations. It was particularly interested in tapping the reservoir of talent that exists far below the elite in Latin America. The difficulties were well-nigh insuperable. First, if substantial numbers were to be recruited, their education would have to start way below the college level. Second, though occasionally qualified students were found, they were invariably deficient in English and needed an additional year here to breach the linguistic barrier.

What is needed is a Linguistic Institute that is highly professional and organized to teach English in cram sessions to any Latin, and Spanish or Portu-

guese to any North American. Such an Institute—
located preferably in Texas or Southern California
—could quickly produce the thousands necessary to
start bridging the great barrier that now exists.

A communications satellite is, of course, a two-
edged instrument. As Dr. Prebisch says:*

> It can be a means of assimilating what is of real
> worth, as well as of transmitting our own contribu-
> tion abroad, if we are properly linked up; or it can
> serve to subordinate Latin American values to oth-
> ers that are highly debatable or definitely prejudi-
> cial to the formation of a genuine culture of our
> own, if in this field—as in that of the economy—
> each country continues to enjoy the privacy of with-
> drawal into its shell, to harbour this odd complex of
> reluctance to co-operate openly.

This is only one aspect of a complicated, multilateral problem in communications. A TV educational program in primary schools and in teacher
training schools, sponsored by AID, has had inter-
mittent success in Colombia. In the long view, the
key is television and a Pan American TV satellite
system serving this hemisphere and dedicated to the
educational and cultural needs of both North and
South America.

Out of my experiences with the attempt to launch
a literacy program in the Dominican Republic grew
a conviction that once we have a Pan American sat-

* *Change and Development*, p. 215.

ellite, people can, at relatively slight cost, organize literacy and other educational programs in agriculture, public health, and the like, in most of the villages of Latin America.

Fourth. Village renovation must begin. High-minded men and women in Latin American nations are eager to start. Mass Education Committees actually exist in some nations. While the educational job must be done by the local people, they need advice and technical help and training from the outside.

Village development programs—designed essentially to build roads, construct bridges, locate and seal springs, erect dams, and build schools and community centers—have been financed by AID. Beyond this is the need to tackle other festering problems of the villages. These villages are worse places for humans than our barns and pens are for cattle and hogs. They have none of the amenities of civilization—no drugs, not even aspirin; no sidewalks; often, no toilets; no schools; no first aid; no refrigeration facilities, let alone medical and dental care. They are miserable sites that often can be smelled at a long distance.

The inhabitants are illiterate and filled with despair, discontent, and disease. The erection of the finest factories in the world will leave them untouched. Yet they contain and condition the most valuable resource of any country—the people.

If Latin America is to have viable societies, as

well as modern ones, these villages must be reno-vated and made into healthy, happy centers where people are enlightened as well as fed and clothed.

The village is, I think, the starting point for the solution of all the problems of Latin America. It will implicate many international agencies.

The first effort to renovate the village was started in the 1930's on the mainland of China by a group headed by James Yen. It never received the blessing of the corrupt and reactionary regime of Chiang Kai-shek but nonetheless it established important pilot projects. In the China Act of 1948, we made provision for financing a Joint Commission on Rural Reconstruction (JCRR) for the renovation of China's villages. This was an international agency, two members being American and three Chinese. It operated in China until it was driven out, and then moved to Taiwan. The burgeoning agricultural economy of Taiwan is due largely to the work of that international agency.

James Yen, who was a member of JCRR, formed a private group which launched this rural recon-struction program in other nations, always working with and through a local indigenous group. The pro-gram is now in force in the Philippines, Colombia, Guatemala, and Thailand.

It has a fourfold thrust:

Health. Water supplies are protected against pol-lution. Sanitary outhouses are built. Screening against flies, pasteurization of milk, boiling of water, and the like, are taught. Vaccinations are given. A first-aid station is set up.

Education. Schools are built, teachers are hired, books and libraries are supplied. Adult literacy courses are established.

Agricultural and Other Livelihood. Modern methods of seed selection, tilling, planting, and spraying are introduced. Crossbreeding is used for improved productivity of chickens, pigs, and other livestock. Fertilizers are introduced. Credit unions and other cooperatives are formed. Handicrafts and cottage industries are introduced.

Civic Action. The villagers are trained and organized for managing the affairs of the village, through village councils and similar groups. They do the planning and policing and provide the general supervision of all local affairs.

Dr. Yen's group soon learned that agricultural technology cannot be exported, because what worked in the temperate zone often failed in a different climate. And so it was that his group established the Institute for Rural Reconstruction in the Philippines, where adaptive research is undertaken and where village trainees from various zones are brought for intensive education.

Dr. Yen always works with a local group in the particular country. In the Philippines it is the Philippine Rural Reconstruction Movement (PRRM). In

[169]

that nation the program is now in about 500 villages, or barrios. This number represents only a small fraction (1.4 percent) of the total number of barrios (almost 30,000) in the Philippines. But those barrios which have been reached are pilot projects whose results are shortly reflected in other barrios. The success of the program caused the Philippine Government to establish a special agency for a national Community Development Program.

The program is implemented by workers who live in the barrios full time for at least two years. They are university- or college-trained graduates. Before they are assigned to the barrios, they undergo training for six months.

As to health, infant mortality in the Philippines has dropped from 101.06 per thousand to 68.05 per thousand, and maternal mortality from 3.7 per thousand to 2.0 per thousand—thanks largely to PRRM.

As to livelihood, the records of production of over 2,000 demonstration farmers in 106 of the barrios show a substantial increase in production and income—again thanks to PRRM. The average annual income per farmer in the region from which the demonstration farmers were selected is about 700 pesos. The average annual income per farmer for the Philippines is only 500 pesos.

The demonstration farmers were shown how to improve their methods of rice culture, engage in hoe gardening, improve the breeds of their native chickens, upgrade their native swine, and produce secondary crops, such as onions and vegetables, on a semicommercial scale. The farmers were urged to undertake these activities during the off-season, when they would otherwise have been idle most of the time.

Many other farmers have followed the practices of the demonstration farmers in modernizing their agricultural methods.

The literacy and self-government programs have had an electrifying grass-roots effect. Historically, under the Spanish system, the Governor of the Province appointed the village government. Now the villages elect their own. Originally all taxes collected in the village were sent to the Province for expenditure. As a result of the growing political consciousness of the villagers, a change was made: now 10 percent of the local revenues are left to the local unit for administration. These two changes required national legislation.

Dr. Yen's program has been in Colombia and Guatemala since 1965. Two sixteen-member teams were sent from each country to the Institute near Manila for training. The Colombian project uses fourteen village workers, the Guatemalan six. In Colombia they work in fifteen villages in the township of Cogua and in a few villages in the townships of Tausa and Nemocur. In Guatemala they work in four villages in the township of San Pedro Pinula and in a few villages in the township of Jolopa and Mataquescuintla. Its pilot project, put into effect late in 1970, is at the village of Santo Domingo.

This village renovation program is now also in Thailand, where it operates in nine villages in four *tambons* (subdistricts) in Charnet Province about one hundred fifty miles from Bangkok.

In each country the projects are only "pilot" projects to show the government and others how to tackle the village problems.

Apart from health projects and educational activities, the two Latin American village programs have inspired home industries whose artisans sell the products on a cooperative basis. There are coffee growers' co-ops; landless *campesinos* have banded together to farm their rented lands; other farmers pool their resources and rent or buy a tractor for use by all; farmers' co-ops are formed that obtain credit to furnish *campesinos* with fertilizers, insecticides, seeds, and the like. Buyers' co-ops have been formed that deal with nonagricultural consumer items. They have as their motto the words of Pope Paul VI, "We are directing ourselves to all the men of good will, conscious that the road to peace passes through development."

The long-range aims of this program are much more than the transformation of miserable villages into places that have a modicum of decency and a few of the amenities of civilization. The aims are basically threefold.

The first is food production. It starts, of course, with the rudiments of diversified agriculture—how to avoid dependency on one crop, how to plan crops in the light of market demands, how to use contour plowing, and where to turn for help when new infestations appear. Beyond this is an introduction to the new technology of the so-called Green Revolution. Rice is a good example. Thanks to the Rockefeller Foundation, a new strain has been developed that works wonders. But it is not available to the subsistence farmers that make up the majority of farmers. A farmer, to enjoy those benefits, needs both knowledge and capital. He needs fertilizers and water, and a way to control pests. That requires foreign exchange. And it is estimated that if the developing nations are to make their subsistence farmers beneficiaries of the Green Revolution, it will require $3 billion of foreign exchange a year. So far in Asia the rich farmer has been the only beneficiary of the Green Revolution. That is why it is said in the Philippines that the Green Revolution may indeed end up as the Red Revolution. In the Philippines Dr. Yen therefore has under way projects designed to offer the small farmers a "package deal" which contains the needed information and the production, marketing, and financing facilities to exploit it. At present there is a bottleneck that will make the rich farmer richer and the poor, poorer.

The second long-range aim relates to the production of people, *viz.* birth control. Dr. Yen knows from his village experience that there is little good achieved in talking to the farmer who spends his day wallowing in the mud with water buffalo. He and his wife are largely impervious to birth control education. The young people, however, are apt students; and, at that level, effective work is done. We also discovered that as the fourfold program develops—health, education, agriculture, and civic action—the standard of living rises and the birth rate tends to drop.

The third aim is land reform. The villagers the world around—the Philippines, Colombia, Guatemala and elsewhere—are sharecroppers who live at the subsistence level.

In Latin America farm laborers have little or no chance of acquiring land of their own. Even when laws require labor contracts, the workers have none, nor do they have any of the protection afforded by them. Rural labor is unorganized except in Venezuela, Bolivia, and Mexico; but in most Latin American countries there are laws barring or restricting unionization of agricultural labor.

About 50 percent of the cash income of Latin American farm workers is spent on food. In some countries there is practically no cash wage, payments being made in kind. In Ecuador the cash wage is about 15 cents a day.

The communists commonly—although not invariably as Yugoslavia illustrates—confiscate the land and turn it into state farms, or collectives. The same tactics were used in Persia where the Shah confiscated the lands of his political enemies and later sold the farms to former sharecroppers. The democratic tradition is otherwise—no class is liquidated; any property taken is paid for. In Ireland state bonds were issued to the landlords. The same was done in Formosa, with the variation that the bonds were issued by a government corporation that invested in industrial companies. The landlords, in general, were happier to have an industrial rather than an agricultural investment.

Once the villagers become literate and aware of the nature of the vise that holds them in bondage, they become promoters of land reform. Nothing of importance has happened to land reform in any country the world over. Ownership changes hands, serfs become landlords, and in time a new feudalism, different only in form from the old, flourishes. In Guatemala land that had been distributed to the peasants was actually returned to the former wealthy owners by the U.S.-supported counterrevolution of 1954. In the Philippines the law on the books reads like a bright promise; in practice it is nothing. The people once were close to having a complete land reform program promised in Luzon Province. But in spite of strong support it was defeated (1) by the Catholic Church and (2) by a Justice of the Supreme Court.

There are bandits, guerrillas, and—if you please —communists in all the lands where Dr. Yen works. But his village level workers, known in the underground as welfare workers, are on lists protected by the bandits; and the uniforms of his workers and the insignia on their vehicles give them immunity from ambush.

The Alliance for Progress gave low priority to village programs. Through its enormous financial resources it nudged a few countries into land reform. But land reform without village renovation can be a sad spectacle. Come with me to Latin America, and I will show you where land reform, which the United States has helped finance, has ended with the members of the establishment getting the choice bottom lands and the *campesino* getting the hilly, inferior top lands. A *campesino* turned loose for the first time on his own is bewildered in his ignorance, and does not know when to plant and when to harvest. As a result, there have been great tragedies. Thus, where sisal is the main crop, the newly liberated villagers are bankrupt when the world price falls. There are no agriculture agents on hand to teach them how to raise substitute crops or how to become diversified farmers.

The complete official village renovation started by Mossedegh in Iran and cut off by United States intervention has taken place in few areas. The most pervasive one is in China, described by Jan Myrdal and Gun Kessle in *China: The Revolution Continued.*

Fifth. Labor-intensive programs—where men, rather than machines, are used—are necessary, pending evolution from the present feudal system to the modern industrial age. We have thought of mechanization as the answer to the agricultural-political problem of producing more and more food. Yet when it comes to food grains the largest output per acre is not in the United States but in Japan and Taiwan, where the laws limit the size of farms to seven and five tenths acres and ten acres, respectively. Mexico has had a similar experience, directing labor on the land to the so-called labor-intensive, high-value crops. The gains in Mexico on these labor-intensive farms have been approximately equal to gains on larger, mechanized units. The social gain was also significant, for labor was used that otherwise would be unemployed and no foreign exchange was expended on imports of high-cost machinery.

Gunnar Myrdal has spoken of the need of "highly labor-intensive" projects in agriculture to take care of employment; and as he points out, this great step forward requires little, if any, expenditure of foreign exchange or, indeed, of capital.*

* 47 *Journ. Farm Econ.* (1965), pp. 889, 898.

In the distant future the machines will, of course, take the place of men. As interim measures, labor-intensive projects, not only in agriculture but in phases of industry as well, are necessary. One tiny example comes from Peru.

There is in Lima a small decorative ceramics industry employing about thirty people. The products are mostly handmade; and the company prospers. It probably could not survive in the United States because of the cost of labor, but in Peru manual labor is often less costly than machines. Until the great factories arrive, the conditions in that ceramics plant tell the present need of Latin America in a compelling way.

To repeat, labor-intensive industries seem to be the greatest need of developing nations, at least in the next decades. Japan, in the emerging pattern of Southeast Asia's development, is "spinning off" traditional labor-intensive industries and helping establish them in regions where there is abundant labor—Taiwan, Korea, Southeast Asia, India. This labor supply is, of course, cheap labor—a third lower than Japan's labor cost. In certain instances, Japan has a wholly-owned subsidiary company engaged in these overseas manufacturing projects. At other times—notably in India—Japan has combined Japanese state enterprise, as well as Japanese private enterprise, with Indian state enterprise. Under pressure, the Japanese show great sensitivity

in meeting the needs and idiosyncrasies of other civilizations and ideologies when negotiating political,
commercial, and business arrangements.

This "spinning-off" of labor-intensive industries
may have merit in this hemisphere as we help design
the future blueprint of industrial and agricultural
Latin America. Some think the place to start is with
textiles, arguing that both we and the Japanese
should specialize in the areas of burgeoning technology.

The Latin sensitivity to United States domination
does not preclude financial, commercial, and business collaboration. Some who speak of this as a pro-
spective "partnership" say it will not be a happy
one, since one partner is overwhelmingly powerful
and the other is abysmally weak. But the inventive
genius of those of this hemisphere is not less than
that of the Japanese; and once the idea of a hemispheric cooperative is fully embraced, there will be
endless potential variations on the means and methods of collaboration between state enterprise and
private enterprise, north and south of the Rio
Grande.

X

Integration of the Hemisphere

The need to integrate the hemisphere—regionally and sectorally.

A discussion of LAFTA and its inadequacies.

The role of CECLA, EEC, and access to markets.

The creation of a hemispheric co-op.

We will get on with our problems and those of Latin America only if we visualize that the solution is a hemispheric one. We should help integrate both the agricultural sectors and the industrial sectors south of the Rio Grande and in time seek for ourselves a place in the new common market. This cannot be done in one law or convention; it will take time and patience and painstaking effort. It can be done and will, I think, be done when it is realized that free enterprise cannot be the solvent of Latin America's woes, that the private sector even in the United States will not be able to give anywhere near full employment, and that the development of the public sector is necessary for our own salvation as well as Latin America's.

This means facing the many perplexing problems of the common market.

The most promising start on the problems of a Latin American common market is the Andean Common Market, which is composed of Colombia, Ecuador, Peru, Bolivia, Chile, and Venezuela. I will discuss it in more detail later.

Five countries in Central America developed a common market (CACM), removing almost all tariff barriers. These five were Guatemala, El Salvador, Honduras, Nicaragua, and Costa Rica. The other nations, except the Guianas, have organized the Latin American Free Trade Area (LAFTA), which has aimed at the reduction of tariffs among member states.

Numerous factors have slowed the progress of LAFTA:

(1) Nationalism, the strongest single force south of the Rio Grande, has dictated that each country develop its own industrial base. This was the origin of the success of Britain, Germany, Japan, and the United States, and it therefore became the model for the rest of the world.

(2) The diverse levels of development meant that a lesser developed nation feared the preemption of its own markets by an aggressive neighbor on its way to industrialization.

(3) There was a fear by the industrial interests in the larger countries that they might be victims of present competitors or of competition by efficient smaller nations.

(4) There was a fear that integration between nations before integration of rural and urban areas within one nation took place, might burden the latter nation.

(5) Managers and owners of newly established industries, safely protected by high tariffs, feared the impact of outside competition for their currently assured market.

(6) The United States has many bastions of strength in Latin American nations, created and bolstered by bilateral financial and business ar-

rangements. From the viewpoint of Latin Americans manning those vantage points, they hesitate to throw their lot in with a regional program where their interests may be secondary. Keeping alive their U.S. contacts may be the better way—at least from the short view.

(7) The United States has reflected hostility toward the so-called benevolent neutralism in most Latin American countries when it comes to international relations. So it has cultivated individual strong-arm, fascist, right-wing groups that will come to our aid in Dominican-type situations. This has led us to be somewhat nebulous when it comes to promoting free trade policies which might evolve into an integrated Latin American economy with a strength sufficient to stand on its own. Moreover, the prospect of a highly protected area flourishing behind the tariff walls of a common market fills some U.S. firms with fear for loss of traditional markets. U.S. protectionist groups, seeing some Latin American manufactured products at a world market price competitive with our own, are filled with alarm, figuring that integration through a common market would further reduce Latin American costs and hurt the United States.

At Punta del Este in 1967, all nations present, including the United States, opted for "the integration of Latin America." Latin America, like other groups of developing countries, would tend to be high-cost producers compared with the mass-producing industrialized nations. But studies have shown that integration with an increase in market size from a national to a regional basis would so lower production costs as to make Latin American costs competitive with world market prices for 12 products out of 14.* While the study is a selective one, it promises much in terms of the hopes and expectations of economic integration.

Dr. Prebisch has wrestled with this problem.** No nation will enter such a system unless it expects that "the benefits of the integration process will be distributed among them in an equitable manner."

And as he points out, "the problem of ensuring an equitable distribution of the benefits of integration is more difficult to solve as between developing than as between developed countries."

Developing countries are not all equal; some are less developed than others. Some may have "within their own borders, large backward areas whose level of development is as low as that of their less advanced partners." That often makes it politically difficult for them to agree to integration with other nations since their own national integration de-

* Grunwald, *Latin American Economic Integration and the United States,* 1969, pp. 11–26.
** *Trade Expansion and Economic Development Among Developing Countries.* TD/B/85 Rev. 1 (United Nations, 1967), pp. 21–22.

serves priority. For a scheme to be "politically nego-
tiable," both the less advanced and the more advanced countries must feel that each would gain
concrete benefits from it.

Public opinion in the associated countries, Dr.
Prebisch says, will not judge the benefits of integration by comparing hypothetical rates of growth, nor
will it easily trust long-term appraisals. What is essential is that "even for the short term there should
be tangible evidence of the benefits of integration,
particularly for the less advanced country. Concrete
manifestations of the new regional group's compre-
hension of the weaker partner's problem are often
indispensable in view of the latter's past experiences. At any rate, probably the most important
reason for the failure of integration schemes or for
the reluctance to enter into them is the insufficient
consideration given to this problem of the fair sharing of the ensuing gains."

The desire and urgency of finding the necessary
common ground were emphasized by the Special
Latin American Coordinating Committee (CECLA)
at its Vina del Mar meeting in 1969. But this committee maintained that for Latin American countries to have viable economies and a viable common market, the industrialized nations of the world
must make concessions. The target of CECLA's
pronouncement at that conference was the elimina-
tion of "the tariff and non-tariff restrictions that im-

pede access to the great world markets under equitable or favorable conditions for the raw, semiprocessed, and manufactured products" of Latin America.

There is a precedent for such policies. The European Economic Community (EEC) has given such preferences to eighteen African nations. In July 1963, the EEC countries and seventeen African states plus Madagascar signed the Yaounde Convention designed to promote an increase in trade between the latter countries—known as the Associated African States and Madagascar (AASM)—and the EEC states. The 1963 Convention of Association gave more meaningful content to the earlier declaration of the EEC countries in the Treaty of Rome, concerning their relations with certain overseas countries or territories.

With respect to trade, the Yaounde Convention provided that there should be created a "zone of free movement for goods adapted to the necessities of these economies which are not yet sufficiently industrialized." In practice, this means three things:

(a) The Associated States have free access to the Common Market, and in return must open their markets to products from EEC states;

(b) The Associated States are permitted (by an express provision of the Convention) to adopt measures to protect their growing economies and infant industries;

(c) The Associated States are free, within quite flexible limits, to participate in the maintenance or establishment of customs unions or free-trade areas among the Associated States or with one or more Third World countries.

Using the first nine months of 1964, 1965, and 1966 as a comparative basis, total imports from AASM countries to EEC states increased by about 16 percent between 1964 and 1966, while total exports from EEC countries to the Associated States increased only at about one-third that rate. The EEC balance with the AASM has always shown a deficit, which increased substantially between 1964 and 1966. Total EEC–AASM trade (imports plus exports) increased about 11.6 percent between 1964 and 1966, the major portion of that increase occurring between 1965 and 1966.

Suggestions have been made that the United States make similar trade concessions to an integrated Latin American economy. If restrictions on agricultural protectionism were removed, it is estimated that about $800 million a year would accrue to the region's earnings.*

More realistically, the drive is on to obtain preferences in the U.S. market for goods from the Latin American common market. The severest of the tariff restrictions are probably placed on refined petro-

* Johnson, *Economic Policies Toward the Less Developed Countries,* Brookings Institution, 1966, pp. 264–265.

leum, refined nonferrous metals (especially copper), pig iron, vegetable oil, and cotton and leather products.* It is estimated that if the United States lowered its various barriers to Latin American manufactures, the latter would increase perhaps $480 million a year. The pros and cons are hotly debated. A convincing argument is made that the money accruing to Latin America would or could be used to purchase machinery and technologically advanced and other sophisticated capital goods from the United States for the developing industrial plants below the Rio Grande.**

My proposal is more pervasive. As I said earlier, the United States should be a part of a hemispheric cooperative. What agricultural and manufactured products should be included in the common market are matters for negotiation. Not everything that each nation produces has a necessary place in such a scheme. To be auspicious, a start should be selective and discriminating. The idea is to lay a base on which in time a full-fledged superstructure can be erected.

This means, in part, the establishment of a common market into which the countries south of the Rio Grande are integrated and which in time the

* Grunwald, *Latin American Economic Integration and the United States,* VII-20.
** A. Maizels, *Exports and Economic Growth of Developing Countries* (Cambridge University Press, 1968), p. 22.

United States may join. All of the fears that Latin Americans have respecting competition from their more developed neighbors are intensified when it is proposed that the United States be a member of such a common market. It is feared that, in that event, we would swamp and kill off the manufacturing and industrial development potential of Latin America. The Latin Americans say that the time may come when the average manufacturing competitive efficiency of the two areas may be sufficiently reduced so that a common market would be possible; but that time, they think, has not arrived.

Perhaps they are right. In any event the first step is the creation of an integrated Latin America with a common market distinguished by local industries turning out the essential products for the masses of people, and locally owned. These new industries might be in the form of free enterprise, though more likely they would be state-owned; or they might be a combination of the two.

XI

A Hemispheric Co-op

Retracing our steps.

The costs as well as the benefits of technology.

The imperative need for an employment policy in industry and in agriculture.

Who will own the new machines?

The functioning of a hemispheric co-op.

Let us retrace our steps. The industrialized nations have saturated the world with packaged goods; and all people now believe that with these packaged goods they too can enjoy the "good life," even though it means jam-packed highways, polluted air, dirty rivers, and a countryside filled with litter. The appeal of the "salesmen" is probably great everywhere, in the slums of the world as well as in the slums at home. For the "salesmen" offer credit. The credit may be oppressive; but the merchandise has glitter, and is irresistible. So are the industrial plants. So is the folklore that surrounds industrialization—the legend that one who envies a strong man should live the regime of the strong man. While industrialization in the U.S., Russian, or Japanese fashion is not necessarily the desirable fate of man, its magnetism is strong. Those who resist and set up planning organizations may escape our most notorious social cancers—Yokohama and Detroit—and create more benign centers. Some nations south of the Rio Grande may indeed be wise enough to create gentle and pleasant alcoves in the Andes, where men may find a decent life with nothing more complicated than a potter's wheel to mark the modern era. But the probabilities are that these alcoves, whether on the Amazon or in the Andes, will be rare. Man's instincts lead him to the machine; and the machine, designed to make men free, in the end can make men prisoners.

The general hypothesis of our system is that people displaced in employment in one sector will find it in another. We are assured that retraining and other such programs will fit them to get jobs perhaps in the labor force engaged in distribution, in the service trades, and so on. But these sectors, which have been growing rapidly and have been absorbing the disemployed from primary and secondary activities, are beginning to fail to serve the employment function.

Most of the new jobs being found are *teaching* jobs, which, of course, are in the public sector. People in the United States are beginning to say: "If we want to give meaning to the Protestant ethic, we had better start revising our concept of what we mean by work. Work and income are the product of what society said had to be done under the circumstances of our one-time economy of scarcity. When the electronic nervous system replaces the human nervous system, then, clearly, in the technological sense, the job is disjoined from income. In other words, the notion that a job is required to qualify and certify a person for income becomes obsolete."

Agricultural technology offers a dramatic example. In this country it produces two kinds of surplus —food and labor. As to the food, there are still hungry people even in the seemingly affluent United States, because we have not solved the distribution problem. It is easy to solve, for it involves only two basic procedures—(a) issuance to the needy of food stamps which may be converted into food at authorized food-stamp stores, and (b) free lunches for schoolchildren. Two paralyzing influences have worked against these programs. First is a species of the Puritan ethic that only hard work and stick-to-it-iveness—not food—make strong people, that breadlines (figuratively speaking) are debilitating institutions; and second is states' rights. States' rights have, of course, been used to clobber blacks into submission, to pass the poor (under guise of vagrancy laws) from county to county and state to state, to keep welfare payments low so as to make entry into a state unattractive, to pulverize farm workers' demands for a living wage, and so on.

States' rights also are the excuse for keeping the poor hungry. Food-stamp programs are not federal but local, in the sense that the Congress has provided that a federally financed food program must originate with the state or one of its agencies. If a state is plagued with poor urban or rural ghettos, the powers-that-be may reckon that the poor will gravitate to Chicago, Pittsburgh, or New York City if things are kept unattractive for them at home. This strategy will gain impetus in some areas if the poor are non-Caucasian. Killing two birds with one stone is an ancient device. As to school luncheons, the school district's decision not to take up a program may be similarly motivated. Moreover, there is ample evidence that, at times, keeping a child hungry is a sadistic weapon aimed at the unpopular views of the parents.

As to the manner in which modern technology produces an excess of labor, there are other forces at work equally degrading to people. A machine can be depreciated; and obsolescence is also a factor of importance in agricultural technology. Depreciation and obsolescence are tax deductions—amounts subtracted from a farmer's gross income before any tax is computed. The more machinery, the greater the deductions.

Labor is not subject to depreciation; only machines are. The taxpayer who is a laborer has no claim to depreciation even in his productive years, for in the economic realm the law glorifies *things,* not *people.* The laborer—every laborer—marches inexorably to the junk pile, no depreciation being allowed him, his wife, or other members of his family.

So we have, under Western philosophy, powerful forces working for machines and against people. Other facts join forces to the same end. Take the Indian in Guatemala who walks all day with a hundred-pound pack of lime on his back from a pit in the hills to a distant processing plant. There is a headband across his brow and he is so bent over with his load that the villagers say he may live to be fifty and never even see the glories of his land, as his eyes are always on the ground. A conveyor belt or a truck is a blessing to this man; and so the appeal of the machine grows and grows.

Man-made systems can be redesigned; ours is not necessarily predestined to rule the earth. But people are people, and the basic drives or motivations are well-nigh universal. In time, I think, the computers will win out as the reasons mount for following the inexorable logic of their teachings. We will in time reach the Age of the Machine—both in agriculture and in operation of the industrial complex. In terms of modern Detroit, Pittsburgh, and Seattle, it will be a Workerless World. Main Street will still exist; the professions and the arts will flourish; schools and hospitals and libraries will operate; social services will greatly expand; sports will flourish, the Age of Literacy will blossom across the world, the seminars and parliaments of men will truly flower, and the Age of the Dialogue will have arrived. But the work of factories will be done by machines. And the basic question—the most critical political issue—will be: Who will own the machines? The answer in Latin America is obviously not free enterprise, for unlike our own system, free enterprise in Latin America has served mostly the elite, not the masses. The answer is likely to be the state or private enterprise in which the state has the dominant interest so that the beneficiaries will be all the people, not a select few.

In the cooperative scheme, each nation should

not be visualized as a miniature industrialized nation largely sufficient unto itself. Most of them are too small to realize that goal. Moreover, the primary market for every industry, in whatever Latin American country it is located, should be the southern hemisphere. Natural resources of a particular nation will largely determine the industries to be located there. So far as I know, no blueprint of such a plan exists. But engineers, economists, and planners can quickly develop one.

The Andean Common Market—composed of Colombia, Ecuador, Peru, Bolivia, Chile, and Venezuela—represents an emerging force working in this direction. One of its main activities is the establishment of a viable internal market for products from industrial plants to be assigned exclusively to the individual nations.

This has involved the development of a free internal market with uniform tariffs. Some 4,000 items are already covered. Plans are being made to put into effect a common external tariff so as to protect the manufacturing units to be established in the various member nations. One nation would allow commodities from an industrial plant in a member nation to enter free import.

The group protects itself from large international corporations. Such companies that manufacture must convert into mixed enterprises with at least 51 percent of their shares in local hands within a set time. Any new foreign investment entering the area must commence with a certain percentage of local shareholders. New foreign investment is not allowed in activities already served by local companies.

As Dr. Prebisch said in his 1970 report, there have been misunderstandings as to what this integration would mean. Thus "there are some who believe . . . that Argentina would have to confine itself to exporting primary commodities to the common market and importing industrial goods. It would be completely irresponsible to think in these terms. With or without a common market, Argentina, like the other Latin American countries, must energetically develop its manufactures and in particular its basic industries. There is no question of returning to the trade pattern of the nineteenth century."

Dr. Prebisch is quite correct. Integration in the sense of the Andean Common Market means making each nation a producer of manufactured goods as well as of foodstuffs.

The Andean Common Market reflects the general direction and thrust of the hemispheric co-op of which I speak. In time there could be a degree of integration between north and south. That would be determined in light of the needs of the integrated common markets south of the Rio Grande.

The plants to be built will be the best that technology can design. In their operation they may use little of the manpower of the continent, as machines will have largely taken the place of men by the time this project is completed. Since the profits from the machines will be enormous, they should inure to the entire community.

The financing will be done in large measure by international agencies such as the World Bank or other creations of the United Nations. These international agencies are parochial; they often finance public agencies in developing nations or cooperatives themselves.

Bolivia is in the bind on tin. After Malaysia it is the second largest tin producer in the world. While the tin mines have been nationalized, Bolivia until 1970 never had a tin refinery of her own. She sold her Bolivian ore abroad; and that put her in another bind, for Anglo-American interests controlled the world's tin market. Under the hemispheric cooperative which I propose, Bolivia would come into its own on tin with adequate tin factories, as well as nationalized mines, and would compete in Latin American markets and in world markets for the sale of these products. Thus she would put her great wealth to use for her own people, rather than for outside interests and outside merchants.

This system of state industries or locally owned industries would be designed to satisfy most of the needs of the consumers of the continent. It would be an integrated whole—leather, food products, textiles, tin, machinery, fertilizers, and all the rest, produced essentially for Latin American markets. This would require a free trade privilege for these state-owned industries which in time will require a continent-wide type of common market.

Many possibilities exist, the form of organization not being critical. OAS—now highly suspect as a U.S. minion—might be vitalized by adding an economic and trade division that supervises the flow of this intracontinental commerce and supplies the adjudicating or arbitral agencies to settle controversies and disputes that are certain to arise.

The cooperative scheme need not be the exclusive method, though it should cover agriculture and the basic industries that produce the essentials of mass consumption.

The job to be done is the admission of the *campesinos* to civilization. Modern technology can create for them the same wealth it has created for us. The problem is to get on with the job before we move any closer to annihilation as a human race.

Removing the United States as the banker and as the policeman will help make this possible. We will remain concerned, and rightfully so. Our technicians will be indispensable in training Latin technocrats.

The Latin American need for scientists and engineers is almost astronomical. Harrison Brown* reports a study made of one typical Latin American

* *Bull. Atomic Sc.* Dec. 1967, p. 6.

nation which, during the next quarter-century, "cannot by any conceivable process meet her needs for highly trained persons in science and engineering." That study concluded that "given adequate assistance from the outside, the country might be able to fill her needs in another 35 to 40 years." The importance of advanced education and training even in agriculture is not commonly appreciated. Harrison Brown reports:* "Japan for example, produces 7,000 college graduate agriculturalists per annum compared with only 1,100 per year in all of Latin America. In Japan there is one farm adviser for each 600 farms. Compare this with perhaps one adviser for 100,000 farms in Indonesia and one adviser per 10,000 farms in Colombia!"

Our business teachers have vast educational tasks ahead of them. So we will be present in force in Latin America with technicians and teachers. But the shadow of the United States will not be across the continent; and there will be no reprisals or threats of reprisal if our bidding is not done.

The United States should join this cooperative venture, establishing industries to round out the hemispheric pattern. These industries would be owned by a public authority that would receive the profits and disburse the dividends.

Population is often called the world's No. 1 problem; and in a sense it is. But once the *campesino*

* *Ibid.,* p. 4.

comes into his inheritance during this age of technology, the birth rate will level off. For the affluent
society tends to stabilize.

Allowing technology—the computer, if you like—
to shape the economic affairs of Latin America is a
relatively easy matter, once the cooperative pattern
is adopted including the agricultural sector and
once it is clear that Uncle Sam and the Marines are
not running the show. Most of the people will rally
behind it provided there is the political restructuring
that is necessary to carry on the new revolutionary
age that will open up. No class will be liquidated or
purged.

Man is on the verge of a new freedom, a release
from manual drudgery. Machines work better in the
production of goods and of most foods than do
men. They work in extremes of cold and heat that
are prohibitive to men. They can perform feats extremely hazardous to a human. They are fast and
efficient and their cost per unit is low. When most
people are not employed in the customary way, vast
new problems are created. The state will provide a
public sector where man can earn his way—a phenomenon that is the destiny of all nations which
create wealth through the use of the new technology.

The creative possibilities for man are now endless. The *campesino* who has never reached fifty
miles beyond his birthplace will become a citizen of

the entire hemisphere. Once the villages are reno-
vated, once the cancers of urban centers are elimi-
nated, humans will come to know and understand
each other. Tensions will decrease. Since there will
be a sharing of wealth and a common realization of
the good life, population as well as the need for warfare and weaponry will decline.

This idea of a cooperative hemispheric order is
today only a dream; but it will unite the oncoming
generation of all these countries in the brightest age
man has known.

Epilogue

W While I think of this book as being about a
hemispheric co-op, it carries that theme
only incidentally. The book deals mainly with the
north–south relationship in this hemisphere—the attitudes, prejudices, and suspicions that each group
has of the other, and the renovations in attitudes
necessary on both sides of the Rio Grande if cooperative, rather than antagonistic, attitudes are to
prevail. Obviously, a hemispheric co-op can be designed and put into operation only under cooperative regimes. Only drastic changes in attitudes will
make that possible. So in a real sense the hemispheric co-op is the secondary theme.

To repeat, we of the north do not have a happy,
relaxed, confident relation with the people south of
the Rio Grande. There are many doubts and suspicions on both sides—some fancied, others based on
bitter experience. We are inclined to think our

southern neighbors are inferior, which of course they are not. They imagine we want to gobble them up which, of course, we do not. The history of this relation has not been what it should be. Though FDR talked about the Good Neighbor Policy, there was much history that had preceded, indicating that we were interveners in our neighbors' affairs and dictators of their policies. We had indeed sent the Marines on many missions with long occupation records. In the 1960's, in spite of our promises and representations, we reverted to type and became the Big Power riding herd on the little Dominican Republic. What we did there to oust Juan Bosch telegraphed itself to sensitive Latin American minds. We were still the imperialists seeking to cow into submission the unorthodox forces south of the Rio Grande.

Our relations with Latin America had in other ways showed veneration for the status quo, the established order, the conservative forces. We were aligned with the elite and the military and never had many avenues of contact with the masses. The elite and military were aligned with the church; and those three made up the conservative triumvirate that ruled the land. Beneath them were the masses trained to believe that though their rewards would come in due course, nothing could be expected until the next life.

Land ownership—the hacienda system—gave the Southern Hemisphere a feudal caste; and in spite of occasional reforms, that old oppressive system held the *campesinos* in a vise.

The masses were effectively excluded from most educational opportunities. They had no medical care, no medical services. They lived like cattle. Their villages were barren of all the amenities of life. Yet because of modern communications they learned from faraway China that it was not necessarily man's fate to be so deprived. Hence in increasing numbers they fled the rural areas, heading for the cities and the bright lights. Thus the miserable circles of slums that surround Lima and Mexico City were formed—the cancers that Mao Tse-tung avoided in new China.

The United States gave financial aid freely, especially under the Alianza, the Alliance for Progress. But most of that aid, though staggering, reached only the elite. In fact, elitism in Latin America has been one of the forces that has made the poor increasingly poorer and made the rich increasingly richer. Industry was mainly built and operated for the elite, not for the masses. The only market for the new units of production were members of the elite who constituted 20 percent of the population. Of the balance, 50 percent lived outside the economy and another 30 percent lived on marginal wages. Industrialization to provide consumer goods for the 20 percent obviously was not a blueprint for development and prosperity.

There were other ramifications of this philosophy. The mainstay of Latin American foreign trade was in the export of commodities—raw materials which were processed by the industrial plants of other nations. Through these exports, Latin America received most of its foreign exchange. This policy fit well the plans of industrialized nations, as they are constantly on the lookout for sources of raw materials to feed their machines. But the dependence on commodity exports is crippling to a developing nation which must manufacture if it wants to put its own people to work and if it is to acquire the foreign exchange worthy of a partner in the world's economic affairs.

Our economic alliance with the elite had its counterpart in our spiritual alliance with the military. Our cold war attitudes made us suspicious of most nonconformists. Our fear that they would use Latin America to undermine our security became an obsession, and that fear was shown not to be baseless by the Cuban missile crisis. As we became more and more involved in Latin American fiscal affairs, the military regimes south of the Rio Grande multiplied. Our counterinsurgency activities increased; and as they mounted so did the suspicions. Hence, we have helped generate an enveloping atmosphere of doubts and suspicions, greatly reducing our effective assistance as good neighbor, scientist, educator, business manager, and even banker.

That is why we must become disengaged from military and counterinsurgency activities and prepare to contribute our vast technical and managerial knowledge to help the developing nations to our south enter the twentieth century.

We must rid ourselves of many preconceptions. Latin America is yet to have its basic revolution that will create the political institutions for a participatory democracy and admit all citizens into regimes of equality and that will make the military subservient.

Private enterprise has served us well; but it has given Latin America a nineteenth-century mercantilism—not inventions, plant building, and merchandising. To reach these goals, Latin America would need the Harvard Business School for some generations.

Latin America has never known the land tenure that Jefferson extolled and that our Congress promoted with the homestead laws. Latin America has never known the family farm. Land reform is sorely needed and, when it comes, the pattern may not be congenial to the Jeffersonian philosophy. But this philosophy cannot be imposed from without. Reform, when it arrives, will be the product of internal convulsions.

Latin America has a great surplus of labor—a condition that theoretically could collide with the automated society promised by our advancing technology. Labor is abundant and cheap and attractive to sweatshop proprietors. Labor despairs, as the people have been taught that "Poverty is the most certain road to eternal felicity." But such teachings today promote rebellions; and the new leaders—men like Raul Prebisch—are soberly counseling that for immediate entry into the twentieth century Latin America needs labor-intensive industries.

Though we are not the most distinguished conservationists in the world, we would nonetheless consider Latin Americans most backward in this regard. Tremendous educational tasks are ahead of those who enter the twentieth century manned with modern technological equipment, if they are to avoid the awful environmental pitfalls awaiting those who take shortcuts.

Education is in many respects the main problem of the people and governments south of the Rio Grande. They are now adopting educational programs tuned to the needs and goals of industrialized nations. It is doubtful if that is the education needed or desirable. Education for village renovation is practically nonexistent.

Literacy is important; and if we create a Pan-American satellite, literacy can easily be the norm for this hemisphere. Education for a sophisticated life in a society such as ours probably misses the mark, for that assumes that Latin America will aim to become an industrialized Europe, Russia, or United States. That depends on the planning and the ideals of the planners.

We are not qualified to make those value judgments. Is Lima or Rio or Santiago to become another Detroit or Pittsburgh? Is the aim to remake Latin America in the image of the West, where consumption of goods—rather than the quality of life—is the goal?

Man lives "not by GNP alone," as Dr. Prebisch has said. There are transcendent values as well, values that the Marxists have largely ignored. And when materialistic standards become the controlling theme, every other value seems to become subordinate.

We, like Russia and Japan, are proponents of the packaged-goods theory of life and living. As a matter of fact, the factories of Europe, Russia, and the United States could produce all the consumer goods that the Latin Americans need. And the temptation of the industrial powers is to work it out that way. But understandably that will not be acceptable to Latin America. So the search for a way to admit them into the inner circle of producers continues.

The search will require financial assistance. But this aid should essentially be granted by multinational agencies such as the World Bank and the

Inter-American Development Bank. And the blueprints of aid for modern agriculture, as well as for the new industrial plants, must come from within if they are to be true to the Latin character and perspective.

Should the aim be to have a car for every family? What about the alternative of mass transportation?

Should the aim be a refrigerator in every house? What about the alternative of a refrigerator for every village, with individual lockers for each family?

Should the aim be the creation of medical and dental schools designed from our blueprints? What of the alternative of local first-aid stations and hospitals everywhere, manned by nurses, midwives, and a scattering of medics?

These problems are typical of the basic planning needed when revolutionary regimes replace the military and the elite. The education needed and the plants required and the degree of specialization decided upon will follow accordingly.

When these preliminary steps are taken, we, as well as they, will be ready for great cooperative undertakings. There may be room for foreign companies in various fields but they will always be dominantly owned by local interests. Each nation will have one or more basic industries whose products will have free access to each other Latin American country. There will be a huge common market. Negotiations must allow us a place in it.

The result will be a disappearance of hunger south of the Rio Grande, and an increasing prosperity and a growing freedom. We will at last be a viable community as relaxed and congenial in our relations to the south as we are with Canada to the north.

It is this kind of sharing that the hemispheric co-op symbolizes. It is, I think, the only way to create a hemisphere of peace and development.

ABOUT THE AUTHOR

WILLIAM O. DOUGLAS was a practicing lawyer in New York City and the state of Washington, a law professor at Columbia and Yale universities and Chairman of the Securities and Exchange Commission. He has been a member of the Supreme Court since 1939. Justice Douglas' hobbies include hiking, conservation, foreign travel and exploration. He is the author of thirty books, including: *Towards a Global Federalism, Russian Journey, Beyond the High Himalayas, Almanac of Liberty, Farewell to Texas.* The present book, *Holocaust or Hemispheric Co-op: Cross Currents in Latin America,* is the third of four volumes dealing with dissent and rebellion. The other two books of the series were *Points of Rebellion* and *International Dissent*; the fourth is *The Three Hundred Years War: A Chronicle of Ecological Disaster.*

GREENVILLE COLLEGE LIBRARY

3 4511 00171 1049

980.03 D74

Douglas, William O. 1898-

Holocaust or hemispheric co-
op: cross currents in Latin